*WELCOME TO
ADULTING
SURVIVAL GUIDE

PREVIOUS TITLES BY AUTHOR

Welcome to Adulting

WELCOME TO ADULTING
SURVIVAL GUIDE

92 Days to Navigate Life

JONATHAN "JP" POKLUDA
WITH VINCE ANTONUCCI

BakerBooks

a division of Baker Publishing Group
Grand Rapids, Michigan

© 2019 by Jonathan Pokluda

Published by Baker Books
a division of Baker Publishing Group
PO Box 6287, Grand Rapids, MI 49516-6287
www.bakerbooks.com

Printed in the United States of America

Library of Congress Cataloging-in-Publication Data is on file at the Library of Congress, Washington, DC.

978-0-8010-9492-7

Unless otherwise indicated, Scripture quotations are from the Holy Bible, New International Version®. NIV®. Copyright © 1973, 1978, 1984, 2011 by Biblica, Inc.™ Used by permission of Zondervan. All rights reserved worldwide. www.zondervan.com. The "NIV" and "New International Version" are trademarks registered in the United States Patent and Trademark Office by Biblica, Inc.™

Scripture quotations labeled NASB are from the New American Standard Bible® (NASB), copyright © 1960, 1962, 1963, 1968, 1971, 1972, 1973, 1975, 1977, 1995 by The Lockman Foundation. Used by permission. www.Lockman.org

Scripture quotations labeled NKJV are from the New King James Version®. Copyright © 1982 by Thomas Nelson. Used by permission. All rights reserved.

Scripture quotations labeled NLT are from the Holy Bible, New Living Translation, copyright © 1996, 2004, 2007, 2013, 2015 by Tyndale House Foundation. Used by permission of Tyndale House Publishers, Inc., Carol Stream, Illinois 60188. All rights reserved.

Some names and details have been changed to protect the privacy of the individuals involved.

The author is represented by The Gates Group of 1403 Walnut Lane, Louisville, Kentucky 40223

19 20 21 22 23 24 25   7 6 5 4 3 2 1

To everyone trying to survive in the real world.
Don't go at it alone.

To Presley, Finley, and Weston.
When you get there, your mom and I are here to help.
I love you all.

✳ CONTENTS

✳ INTRODUCTION

As I was working on my book *Welcome to Adulting*, I hit a difficult spot. The book took off, which was cool, but I never anticipated it being so successful. Suddenly I found myself being invited to speak at more conferences and churches. At the same time my job responsibilities were changing, and I lost a valued coworker, which put even more responsibility on me. A loved one got sick while our kids' activities cranked up. It was all too much and, for the first time in my life, I began experiencing anxiety.

The good news is that there is a lot of help out there for someone who is struggling. The bad news is that I didn't know what help to choose. The options were overwhelming, and I almost felt like that increased my burden.

Simplicity

Finally, I found what worked for me. *Simplicity*. Every morning I focused on just one idea. I contemplated that idea, I meditated on it, and I looked to apply it that day. That simple focus helped me to survive that day. Soon I was out of the woods, no longer just hoping to survive but seeking to thrive in the abundant life Jesus offers his followers.

My prayer is that this book can provide the same help for you. You'll find the format is similar to what I needed. There is one short, focused reading per day for the next six weeks. Each day you'll also find a Bible passage to read, a question, an application, and a prayer. I hope this helps you put one foot in front of the other, allowing you to walk a path of faithfulness in the uncharted territory of adulting.

Real-Life Scenarios

Have you seen the survival guide for "worst-case scenarios"? It teaches you how to survive an anaconda attack and an avalanche. The chapters are interesting and humorous, but they present circumstances the average young adult will never find themselves in.

The book you hold in your hands (or are looking at on your electronic device) is filled with situations you *will* find yourself in. For each, you will find biblical advice based on a biblical worldview.

Pattern Recognition

For over a decade, I had the privilege of being the pastor of the largest young adult gathering in America. I've been able to observe the lives of tens of thousands of young adults. Watching that many people, I started to recognize patterns. I saw some choices that led to devastation and others that led people to move successfully into young adulthood.

I want to help you make wise decisions that honor God and put you on a path of not just surviving but thriving. My goal is that the truth of Proverbs 16:3 will become a reality in your life. "Commit to the LORD whatever you do, and he will establish your plans."

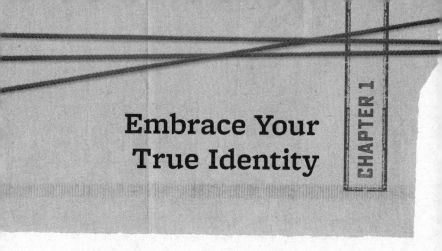

CHAPTER 1

Embrace Your True Identity

Therefore, if anyone is in Christ, the new creation has come: The old has gone, the new is here! –2 Corinthians 5:17

When I was a kid, I lived on a farm. One day, my dad asked me to get him the fence stretcher.

"The fence stretcher?" I asked.

My dad explained exactly where I would find it in the garage. I ran to the spot and looked, but no fence stretcher. I went back and told my father he was wrong. I explained, "The only thing there is my toy machine gun."

My father gave me a confused look and started walking toward the garage, where he picked up . . . my toy machine gun. He showed it to me. "This is a fence stretcher."

I gave my father a confused look. I wanted to explain to him that, no, what he was holding was the make-pretend machine gun that I had used countless times to shoot make-pretend bad guys. But I didn't. I decided my father was wiser than me and was probably right.

Me

When I was a kid, I was thought of as a "future farmer."

In my teens, as I got my ears pierced and got a tattoo, I became a "rebellious future farmer."

In college, I became a "partier."

After college, I started to pursue money and respect and I became "successful."

The whole time, I didn't have much interest in God. I would show up at church (I'm from Texas, where nearly everyone shows up at church), but I didn't have much to do with God. It was easy. Why would a rebellious, partying, successful guy want to have anything to do with God? And, I thought, why would God want to have anything to do with a rebellious, partying, successful guy?

Then I started hanging out with some people who were really different. They were real, and fun, and caring, and cool. They were Christians.

They gave me a different way of looking at God. I discovered that he was a loving Father. I also learned that I was God's beloved child. I wanted to explain to him that, no, I was actually a rebellious, partying, successful guy. But I didn't. I decided my heavenly Father was wiser than me and was probably right.

Suddenly it didn't make sense for me to not have interest in God or to ignore him. I was his child, I was loved, and I wanted to live my life in relationship with him.

You

If I asked, "Who are you?" how would you answer?

You might tell me your name, which is a nice sound your parents assigned to you, but it is not your identity.

If you're in school, you might say, "I'm a student," but what happens after you graduate?

Similarly, defining yourself by what you do, like your job title, only describes what you currently do for about forty hours a week. It's not who you are.

There are other ways you might define yourself: by your hometown, your college degree, or a state championship you won, or as a "foodie" or a "shopaholic." You might get hung up on something you've done in the past that you regret or that hurt you or others: you're an ex-con, a divorcée, someone who had an abortion. But, again, that's not who you are.

True You

When I was in college, before I became a Christian, one night I wanted to get into a bar in Dallas. I was underage but I had a plan. My roommate was twenty-one, and I would use his ID.

I confidently walked up to the bouncer and handed him the ID.

He looked at it, looked at me, and started shaking his head. "It says here that you're five-foot-nine."

I am six-foot-seven, so this wasn't looking good. But I tried to play it cool. "That's a typo," I replied. "I'm five-nineteen." (If you do the math, that actually works out to six-foot-seven. I'm a genius!)

He looked at the ID again and read the name, "Babak Ali Hadid."

I hadn't considered the fact that my roommate was Iranian and I was . . . not.

My plan didn't work. My true identity betrayed the fake me I was trying to be. I was no more a five-foot-nine Iranian than my dad's fence stretcher was a machine gun.

My hope is that your true identity will betray the fake you. Because no matter what you've been told about you, no matter what you think about you, the truth is, you are God's beloved child. If you understand and embrace your true identity, it will change not only the way you think of yourself but your entire life.

Think of it this way: Why does a caterpillar crawl around in the mud? Because it's a caterpillar. But then a caterpillar goes through a transformation process in which it becomes a new creation; it becomes a butterfly. A butterfly flies through the sky. Why? Because it's a butterfly. If you saw a butterfly crawling in mud, what would you have to assume? That butterfly still believes it's a caterpillar!

You are not who you think you are, and you are not who you were. If you have put your faith in Jesus, you are a new creation. You are God's beloved child. When you understand that, you will no longer crawl in the mud. Why would you? You can fly.

PONDER

How do you think embracing your true identity would change your life?

PRACTICE

Commit to going on this survival guide journey for forty-two days. You'll read each day's entry and then pray. Remember, you're God's child praying to your heavenly Father. Nothing makes more sense than that! You were made for this!

PRAY

God, I want to know you for who you truly are, a perfect, loving Father. I want to know who I truly am, your beloved child. I want to have a relationship with you based on who I truly am, and I want to live out my true identity every day. Please help me.

CHAPTER 2

Recovery

> Therefore confess your sins to each other and pray for each other so that you may be healed. The prayer of a righteous person is powerful and effective. –James 5:16

I have a large scar on my chest. I told my kids I was shot with a bow and arrow. You should've seen how big their eyes got as they realized they had the coolest dad in the world.

The truth is, I had a mole cut off and it left a big, gnarly scar.

My guess is that you have some scars. I don't mean scars on your skin. I'm talking deeper. You have been wounded by others, and some of the hurts you have suffered have been self-inflicted. All of it has messed you up and creates problems for other people with whom you have relationships.

Before coming to Christ, I drank heavily and had tried cocaine, ecstasy, and other drugs. But thankfully, I was able to quit immediately and the scars seem minimal.

Unfortunately, I can't say the same about pornography. I was enslaved. Before becoming a Christian, I was so deep in my addiction

I would call in sick to work so I could stay home and binge-watch porn. After becoming a Christian, I continued to be tempted. My past with porn was impacting my present, and I needed to be free.

If your past is choking the life out of you, if you're drowning in sin, what you need is CPR.

Confess (C)

When we feel stuck in our past, in our sin or pain or addiction, we come up with all kinds of solutions, but God has already told us what to do: *confess*.

We confess to God: "If we confess our sins, he is faithful and just and will forgive us our sins and purify us from all unrighteousness" (1 John 1:9).

And we confess to faithful friends: "Therefore confess your sins to each other and pray for each other so that you may be healed" (James 5:16).

After making those initial confessions, you may find you are not yet healed or purified. What do you do? You keep confessing but move it to the thought level. Instead of just confessing after you've sinned, start confessing *before* you sin. Make a game of it. Confess as soon as you sense the temptation. Confess when your mind starts moving in the direction you don't want it to go.

Pray (P)

We live in a very self-help culture, but self is not the answer to your problems. Self is what got you in trouble in the first place.

God is the answer, and so you need to take the problem to him. You need to *pray*.

Pray honest, desperate prayers. Tell God exactly what's going on and exactly how you're feeling. Tell him when you want to click on a website, buy more clothes that you don't need and can't afford, or are tempted to eat or drink something you swore you wouldn't.

I finally began experiencing recovery from my porn addiction because of confession and honest, desperate prayers. Throughout my day I would plead with God, "Please don't let me click on that hashtag." "Please don't let me wonder what color underwear she has on."

To find freedom, beg God to help you take every thought captive and make it obedient to Christ (see 2 Cor. 10:5).

Repent (R)

You've spoken the sin out loud to others. You've asked them to pray, and you've prayed like your life depended on it. What's left? *Repentance*.

Some people think repentance is being sorry for something you've done—really, really sorry. It's not. To repent means to turn around. You realize you've been going the wrong way, so you turn around.

You turn away—and run from—your sin. God tells us that repeatedly in 1 Corinthians 6:18, "Flee from sexual immorality," in Amos 5:14 (NLT), "Run from evil," and in 2 Timothy 2:22, "Flee the evil desires of youth." Confession and prayer are helpful, but when temptation strikes, run!

One aspect of turning away from sin is removing access to it. Jesus told us,

> If your right eye causes you to stumble, gouge it out and throw it away. It is better for you to lose one part of your body than for your whole body to be thrown into hell. And if your right hand causes you to stumble, cut it off and throw it away. It is better for you to lose one part of your body than for your whole body to go into hell. (Matt. 5:29–30)

What would it look like for you to remove access to whatever might lead you into sin? I've had guys approach me after hearing me talk about my porn addiction and say, "I'm struggling like you did."

I always ask, "How do you access porn?"

Inevitably, the guy will answer, "My phone."

Then I ask, "Where's your phone?"

This dude will look at me suspiciously and say, "In my pocket."

I have to tell him, "You're not struggling with porn. You're carrying it around with you in your pocket. You haven't even begun to struggle."

If something is killing you, don't carry it around with you! Am I really asking that guy to get rid of his cell phone? Yes, I am. "Get a flip phone, bro. Your life will go on, with more life in it." Do whatever it takes to remove access.

To repent, you turn away and run from sin, and you turn and run *to* Jesus. The way to remove the power of a temptation is to understand that Jesus—and what Jesus is offering—is better.

Today, God has given me freedom, but back when I was still a slave to porn I would drive home from work every day looking forward to seeing a billboard near my house that featured a scantily clad girl advertising an adult bookstore. But through confession and prayer, I grew in my intimacy with Jesus. The more I had of him, the more I desired more of him. One day I drove home from work and I didn't want to look at the billboard. *It's not worth it*, I thought. I wanted Jesus more.

Whatever you're struggling with, Jesus is greater. Whatever tempts you, Jesus is better. Confess, pray, and repent. Be revived with CPR.

PONDER

Read this sentence out loud, filling in the blank: I'm addicted to

_____ .

PRACTICE

It's time to start the CPR process by confessing. It's scary, but you'll be glad you did. Confess your sin to God and to a trusted group of believing friends.

PRAY

Father God, thank you that if I confess my sins to you, you will forgive me. You know me. You know my sin. I confess it to you. I am sorry. I accept what Jesus did for me on the cross. God, I don't want to sin against you anymore. Help me.

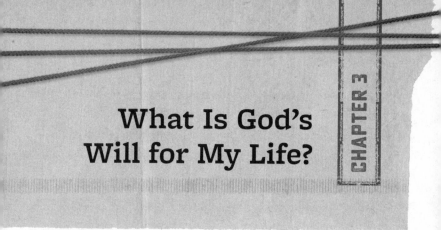

CHAPTER 3

What Is God's Will for My Life?

Take delight in the LORD, and he will give you the desires
of your heart. –Psalm 37:4

I've been a pastor to people in their twenties and thirties for a
while now, and one question I often hear is, "What is God's will
for my life?" People might ask it because they're wondering about
career decisions, who they should date, or whether they should
move.

What Scripture Says

I always ask if they know the Bible clearly tells us God's will for
our lives. For instance:

- "For my Father's will is that everyone who looks to the
  Son and believes in him shall have eternal life." (John
  6:40)
- "It is God's will that you should be sanctified: that you
  should avoid sexual immorality; that each of you should

learn to control your own body in a way that is holy and honorable, not in passionate lust." (1 Thess. 4:3–5)

- "Rejoice always, pray continually, give thanks in all circumstances; for this is God's will for you in Christ Jesus." (1 Thess. 5:16–18)

These verses are pretty straightforward. We should look to Jesus for eternal life, avoid sin and sexual immorality, rejoice always, pray continually, and give thanks in all things.

But What I Really Want to Know

At this point the person asking will inform me that what they are looking for is more specific direction.

I get that, but sometimes the person asking is willfully ignoring what God's already been clear on. They want to know God's will for some specific issue when they have proven they're not willing to obey what God has already told them. If you aren't listening to what God has already said, why should he bother saying anything else to you?

If you *are* listening to what God has already said, I think he might give you more direction, and you would be better able to discern what he's telling you. The Bible says that too, in Romans 12:2. "Do not conform to the pattern of this world, but be transformed by the renewing of your mind. Then you will be able to test and approve what God's will is—his good, pleasing and perfect will."

Freedom and Backyard Boundaries

The main thing I tell people who are asking how to discern God's will for some decision is that they don't need to. They don't need to because part of God's will was to give us free will. Beyond the basic guidelines he's given us in Scripture, he wants us to have the freedom to make our own decisions.

When my kids were younger, and before they could swim, they loved to play in the backyard. It had a play set with a slide, monkey bars, a seesaw, and a tree fort. I'd tell them to go for it and to have fun—but to stay within the fence and away from the pool. Those boundaries were for their safety. Within those boundaries, they didn't have to ask because they could do what they wanted.

They would still ask, because they'd forget their options and get paralyzed by indecision. Soon, they'd be shouting.

"Daddy, can we go down the slide?"

"Sure. Just stay within the fence and away from the pool."

"Daddy, should we go down the slide or play on the monkey bars?"

"Baby girl, do what you want. Just stay within the fence and away from the pool."

"Daddy, can we play in the street?"

"Of course not, because it's not within the fence."

Do as You Please

There's a quote that's been attributed to an early Christian theologian named Augustine: "Love God and do what you please." This might sound like bad theology, but Jesus said if we love God we will do what he commands (see John 14:15). If we're doing what God commands, what he's told us in the Bible, then we can do what we please. God's given us that freedom, and if we love God, what we do will please him.

PONDER

If you've been assuming God has a specific will for an area of your life, perhaps he's given you the freedom to do what you think is best. How could that perspective change how you proceed?

PRACTICE

What choice are you facing that this new approach could impact? Why don't you make a decision and start moving in that direction?

PRAY

God, I want to do your will for my life. Help me to know where you have a specific path for me and where you have given me the freedom to choose. Please help me to always live in your wisdom.

Questions to Ask When Navigating a Gray Area

"I have the right to do anything," you say—but not everything is beneficial. "I have the right to do anything"—but not everything is constructive. No one should seek their own good, but the good of others. –1 Corinthians 10:23–24

Should you go to your friend's bachelor party?

A guy asks you out; should you say yes?

You start dating, and you know you can't have sex before marriage, but is kissing OK?

You're in Las Vegas for a wedding; is it OK to gamble a little?

In many areas—more than most people today want to admit—what's right and wrong *is* clear. God gives absolute truth, and Christians should absolutely live by it. Christians should not sin, not just because it's "the rules" but because sin leads us away from God, life, and happiness.

But what about those areas that are not so clear?

It's very clear that you should not become drunk (see Eph. 5:18), but should you drink at all? And can you hang out with people who are getting drunk?

It's clear that you should only date people who share your faith, but if there are two people you're interested in, and they both share your faith, which one do you ask out?

You can't live together with someone you're dating, but if you go visit your friends who are living together, is it OK to spend the night at their place?

When I was working in corporate America in Dallas, a friend of mine in Waco offered me the position of vice president of his company. It would be a big step forward in my career and include a fat raise. I didn't know what to do. I searched the Bible, but the words "Dallas," "Waco," "vice president," and "raise" do not even make an appearance. I wanted to do God's will but could not discern what it was.

Christians call these decisions we need to make where God has not spoken directly "gray areas." What do you do when the answer is not black-and-white? I have a list of seven questions I pray through to help me navigate a gray area.[1]

1. Will It Have Negative Long-Term Consequences?

Don't do it—whatever it is—if it will have negative long-term consequences. We live in an instant gratification society. "If you want to, do it!" "If it will feel good, do it!" The problem is that what feels good in the moment is often not what's best for your future. You need to remember that the decisions you make today will determine who you are tomorrow. With each choice you are becoming something. Every decision has consequences.

You need to ask, Will it have negative long-term consequences? An obvious example is taking on unwise consumer debt. If you buy that big-screen TV for $2,000 but can only afford to make the minimum payments on your credit card, you're going to end up paying well over $3,000 for it.

2. Could It Harm My Body?

The Bible says your body belongs to God and is his temple, so if what you're considering could harm your body, don't do it.

Some choices seem obvious. Shooting up drugs, even just once, would defile your body (see 1 Cor. 6:12–20). For those areas that are less clear, moderation may be the way to go. For instance, smoking a cigar once in a while might not be a problem, but smoking them every day could lead to cancer.

3. Will It Give Me a Guilty Conscience?

You should not do whatever you are considering if it will you give a guilty conscience.

Back in Bible times, there was disagreement about whether Christians should eat meat that had been sacrificed to idols. So, was it kosher (pun intended) to eat it or not? The answer was, it depends . . . on your conscience. "But whoever has doubts is condemned if they eat, because their eating is not from faith; and everything that does not come from faith is sin" (Rom. 14:23).

If you think something is wrong, it *is* wrong for you. If someone else doesn't think it's wrong, it's not wrong for them.

4. Will It Cause Someone Else to Sin?

When the early Christians were debating whether it was permissible to eat meat sacrificed to idols, the answer was it depends on your conscience . . . *unless* it might cause someone else to sin. Christians were instructed that if they felt the freedom to eat the sacrificed meat they could, unless they were with another Christian who did *not* feel free to eat the meat. If they ate the meat it might lead the other Christian to do the same and violate his or her conscience (see 1 Cor. 8:9–10).

If you have the freedom to do something but it could cause someone else to sin, don't do it.

For example, if I feel the freedom to have a glass of wine but I am having dinner with a friend who is a recovering alcoholic, I should give up my freedom and not drink, so there's no temptation for my friend to join in.

5. Will It Hurt My Witness?

We don't want to hinder the spread of the gospel, and you never know who may be watching, so if it might hurt your witness, don't do it. We want our lives to be different and stand out in a way that causes others to ask questions (see 1 Pet. 3:15–17).

If the answer to those five questions is no, then it seems like it's not a bad idea. But is it a *good* idea? To determine that, ask yourself these final two questions.

6. Will It Benefit Myself or Others?

The thing you are considering doing may not have a negative impact, but as followers of Jesus we don't want to just avoid what's wrong; we want to do good. Ask, Will it benefit me? Will it benefit others? If not, maybe find something else that will make God's world a better place.

7. Will It Bring Glory to God?

When I was offered the better job in Waco, I didn't know if I should take it. I sought wisdom from a guy who was discipling me. I needed to know, What's God's will?

He asked, "If you go to Waco, and you are wildly successful, and the company goes public, and you make a ton of money, was it God's will?"

"Yeah," I answered, "I guess so."

"If you go to Waco," he asked, "and you don't do well, the company goes under, and you lose your job and end up homeless, was it God's will?"

I said, "No, probably not."

"You're approaching this all wrong," he told me. "You can't judge obedience by the outcome. God's in charge of the outcome. You're in charge of obedience. What you need to decide is where you can glorify God the most. Which will help you seek him, grow spiritually, and best honor him with your life? The answer to that question is the answer to what you should do. And if you don't know the answer to that question, you have the freedom to choose."

He was right. Ultimately, the purpose of our lives is to glorify God. We need to do what we think will best help us accomplish that purpose.

For me, I decided I could grow the most spiritually by staying in Dallas so I could continue to attend Watermark Church.

What will allow you to glorify God the most?

PONDER

What gray area are you struggling to navigate?

PRACTICE

Whatever decision you're facing, use the seven questions to pray through it.

PRAY

God, thank you for giving me freedom. Help me to never use my freedom to sin or in a way that might make you look bad. When I don't know what to do, help me to always look to you and make the wise choice.

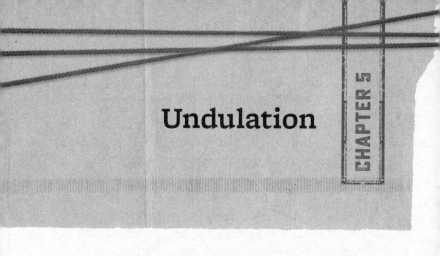

CHAPTER 5

Undulation

We are not like Moses, who would put a veil over his face
to prevent the Israelites from seeing the end of what was
passing away. –2 Corinthians 3:13

Have you ever looked around at a church service at everyone
praying or passionately singing songs to God and felt like
you were the only one not feeling it? Or, even worse, you remembered when you had that kind of fire but realized it has faded?

If you've been there or are there, can I tell you as a pastor what
I think about you? You are *normal*.

The Law of Undulation

The Bible tells us that Satan has a well-devised strategy to pull
people away from faith in God, and we need to be aware of his
schemes (see 2 Cor. 2:11 and Eph. 6:11). In his book *The Screwtape
Letters*, C. S. Lewis imagines a dialogue between a senior demon
and the junior demon he's training in the art of tempting humans.
They call humans the "patients."

At one point the senior demon talks to the junior demon about the "law of undulation."

> Undulation: The repeated return to a level from which they repeatedly fall back. A series of troughs and peaks. If you had watched your patient carefully you would have seen this undulation in every department of his life—his interest in work, his affection for his friends, his physical appetites, all go up and down, up and down. As long as he lives on earth, periods of emotional and bodily richness and liveliness will alternate with periods of numbness and poverty.[1]

I think C. S. Lewis is right. The demons know about the law of undulation, but they don't want you to know. That's why you hear those whispers.

When you are at the top of your peak you hear, *Look at you, you are a Super Christian! You can conquer anything. You don't have to worry about temptation anymore.* You start getting full of yourself, and that is not good.

Then, when you're down in the troughs, the tune changes. *Look at you, you're not even a real Christian. That's why God doesn't really love you.*

No. This is normal. It's undulation. It happens to all of us. We experience the mountaintop then find ourselves down in the valley.

The Veil

Moses used to spend face-to-face time with God in what was called the tent of meeting (see Exod. 34). When he came out, he would be glowing. People could see that he had spent time with God. But over time, that glory would fade. We are told, later in the Bible, that Moses would put a veil over his face. Why? He didn't want people to see the glory of God fading from him.

I think we do the same thing. Like Moses, we tend to put a veil over our fading glory because it's embarrassing. No one wants to go up to their friend and say, "No . . . I'm not as excited about God as I was when I talked to you two weeks ago." So, like Moses, we wear a veil.

We don't wear a literal veil. What Christians do is wear the veils of smiles and denials. When people ask, "How are you doing?" we answer, "Good! I'm fine. Everything is good." It's not, but we hide behind a veil. Right? "It's another new day with God! His blessings are new every morning! God is good, all the time. And all the time, God is good!"

Now, if you are really feeling that way, I suppose there's nothing wrong with expressing it. In fact, authentic joy and enthusiasm for God can be contagious, so if you are really feeling that way, stand next to me.

I'm not saying there's anything wrong with being that way if you're really feeling it. What I am saying is that if you are *not* really feeling it, don't fake it. And no one feels that way all the time.

It's dangerous if Christians fake it, because then they can't get help when they're down. It's also dangerous for other Christians, because they see this person who seems to always be up and they start to question their own Christianity. *Why do I sometimes feel down? Why don't I always feel so close to God? Why isn't it always easy*

for me to praise God? What's wrong with me? What am I doing wrong?
But there's nothing wrong with the person who's experiencing ups
and downs. They're just undulating. What's wrong is the Christian
who's wearing a veil.

Don't fake it. When the glory fades, be honest. Share how you're
really doing with some people who care about you. They'll be re-
lieved they're not alone, and you will get support.

PONDER

When you feel like you've "fallen" far from God, is it possible that
part of the reason is because you're not doing "the things you did
at first" (Rev. 2:5)?

PRACTICE

Do you have some trusted friends you can talk to about feeling far
from God? Why don't you talk to them about the law of undulation
and how you've experienced it?

PRAY

God, I always want to feel close to you, but I don't always feel close
to you. When the glory fades, help me to be honest with you and
with my friends. And, God, please always pull me back to you.

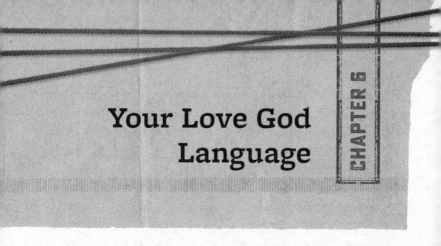

CHAPTER 6

Your Love God Language

And I pray that you, being rooted and established in love, may have power, together with all the Lord's holy people, to grasp how wide and long and high and deep is the love of Christ, and to know this love that surpasses knowledge—that you may be filled to the measure of all the fullness of God. –Ephesians 3:17–19

What's your love language? What can a person do to make you feel loved by them?

The Love Languages

In 1995, Gary Chapman came out with a book called *The Five Love Languages*. In it, he explains that people experience love in different ways. For some, receiving gifts gives them all the feels. Others feel more loved when someone serves them. Or it could be spending quality time together, words of affirmation, or physical touch.

My love language is receiving gifts. Buy me something and I'll receive that as love. Because I experience love best through gifts, it's also natural for me to want to express my love by giving gifts. So if I want my wife to feel special, I'll buy her something. But my wife's love language is acts of service. Receiving a gift doesn't do much for her; she wants me to mow the lawn. Washing the dishes is a romantic gesture for my wife.

Of course, I need to express my commitment to my spouse in all five ways. My wife's top love language is not words of affirmation, but that doesn't mean I never tell her I love her. And just because gifts don't do much for her doesn't mean I don't give her a present on her birthday. But what it *does* mean is that whatever love language my partner has, I should focus on speaking that love language.

The Love God Languages

Jesus was once asked to name the most important commandment. He answered, "Love the Lord your God with all your heart and with all your soul and with all your mind and with all your strength" (Mark 12:30). What God wants from us, and for us, is love. To be filled with his love, and to be filled with love for him.

How can a person experience God's love and express their love for him?

There are many "love God languages."

Just knowing God and getting to know him more grows our love for him. Reading God's love letters, the Bible, helps us to love God more. Talking to God, honestly and intimately, will deepen our relationship with him. That's why prayer isn't just a before meals and bed checklist item but an essential piece of life with God.

When you first start dating someone, one way you show your affection and grow your relationship is by taking an interest in what they're interested in. If you want to love God more, start seeking to care about what he cares about.

Jesus told us that we reject God when we disobey him, but obeying him is a way we live life in his love (see John 14:15).

Your Love God Language

I sometimes ask people, "What makes you love God more?" Most don't have an answer. Some have been around church long enough that they dutifully give the "right" answer, "Reading my Bible," whether it's true or not.

What makes me love God more is . . . a little weird. I "take delight in the LORD" (Ps. 37:4) by taking a bath. Why is that where I best experience God's love and express my love for him? I think it's because the bathtub is a place where I can get away from my three young kids and from technology. I love my kids and technology, but they can distract me from focusing on God.

I've talked to people who grow their love for God by being out in nature. I have friends who listen to and sing along with worship music. For others it's spending quiet time with him on the porch over a cup of coffee in the morning.

What about you? What stirs your affection for God? You need to know the answer to that question.

If you are in a relationship with God, you need to experience his love and express your love for him in all different ways, but you should focus on speaking your "love God language."

PONDER

When have you felt closest to God? What were you doing?

PRACTICE

Start experimenting with different ways to connect with God today. Take a bath, go on a walk, sing some worship songs, get out in nature. Find your love language.

PRAY

God, thank you for loving me! I want to love you more and more. **Help** me to know and respond to your love for me. Help me to do the things that will grow my heart for you.

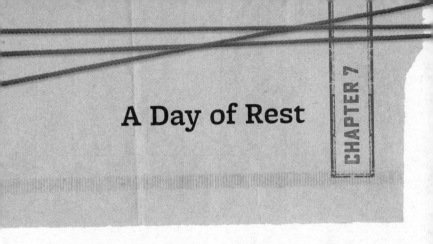

A Day of Rest

> By the seventh day God had finished the work he had been doing; so on the seventh day he rested from all his work. Then God blessed the seventh day and made it holy, because on it he rested from all the work of creating that he had done. –Genesis 2:2–3

God rested on the seventh day, and on each seventh day of our six-week journey, I will give you a day of rest from reading a chapter.

However, we do not rest *from* God. We rest with God and for God. I hope you will use these days of rest to be filled with God.

Yesterday you received the assignment of experimenting with different "love God languages." Why don't you try one of those today?

CHAPTER 8

Let Your GPS Guide You

> Just as a body, though one, has many parts, but all its many parts form one body, so it is with Christ. For we were all baptized by one Spirit so as to form one body—whether Jews or Gentiles, slave or free—and we were all given the one Spirit to drink. –1 Corinthians 12:12–13

I had the honor of leading the largest gathering of young adults in the country for over a decade. If you look at the epicenter of every revolution you will find young adults—the French Revolution, the American Revolution, the Sexual Revolution, the Pop-Tart Revolution. (I can't believe how many flavors of Pop-Tarts there are now!)

I especially love today's young generations because they want to make a difference in the world. That's awesome, because God made us to make a difference. "For we are God's handiwork, created in Christ Jesus to do good works, which God prepared in advance for us to do" (Eph. 2:10).

If you want to make a difference, the question becomes, How can you make the *biggest* difference with your life? A lot of young adults are asking that question. My advice? Follow your GPS.

Follow Your GPS

I am completely directionally challenged. I am always as lost as an Easter egg. I get lost going to my house. Literally!

Because I often can't figure out the way to go, I rely on my GPS. At times I have challenged my GPS. My GPS has told me to go in a certain direction, but, confident I was right, I went the opposite way. Every time I've done this, I've been wrong. The GPS is always sending me in the right direction.

God has built you with a GPS. If you follow it, it will show you where to serve and how to make the biggest difference with your life.

Gifts (G)

You have spiritual gifts. God gives every Christ-follower talents they are to use to serve others and impact the world. Different spiritual gifts are listed in 1 Corinthians 12:7–11 and Romans 12:6–8. These gifts include teaching, serving, giving, leadership, administration, hospitality, and wisdom.

How do you know which gifts God has given you? I would encourage you to experiment. Try serving in different ways. Take note of the things you're pretty good at and where you receive positive comments from others on your ability.

Start examining yourself, seeking to discern what God has made you great at. Is it easy for you to talk to strangers about spiritual topics? You may have the gift of evangelism. Do you enjoy reading and explaining the Bible? You might have the gift of teaching. Do you enjoy having people over and making sure they are well cared for and comfortable? You could have the gift of hospitality.

You get the picture. God has given you gifts to serve him and others. Do you know what they are?

Passion (P)

What are you passionate about? It might be working with children, caring for the elderly, helping the homeless, investing in the lives of teenagers, or seeing new Christians grow spiritually.

There's something you care deeply about that God also cares deeply about. That passion area is God-given and probably where you should deploy your gifts.

Story (S)

We've all been shaped by our past. We have a mix of good and bad experiences that come together to form our story. Those experiences allow us to relate to, understand, and give advice to others going through something similar.

God loves to bring good out of bad. Almost every ministry I can think of was started because of someone's story. A man who struggled with addiction starts a twelve-step recovery ministry. A woman who healed from the pain of divorce starts to counsel women whose husbands have left them. A man who went to jail starts a prison outreach ministry. A woman who had an abortion gets the courage to speak about it and ends up starting an abortion recovery group. God will take your mess and make it your message.

How do you make the biggest difference with your life? Follow your GPS.

PONDER

What does your GPS tell you about where you should serve and make a difference?

PRACTICE

Text a couple of Christian friends explaining that you are trying to discern your spiritual gifts and where you should be serving. Ask them what they have seen in you.

PRAY

God, what an honor that you have gifted me to serve—thank you! Please help me to understand and serve according to the unique way you made me. I want to make the biggest impact I can for you.

CHAPTER 9

Compounding Interest

Do not be deceived: God cannot be mocked. A man reaps what he sows. Whoever sows to please their flesh, from the flesh will reap destruction; whoever sows to please the Spirit, from the Spirit will reap eternal life. –Galatians 6:7–8

People who live amazing lives—how did they get there? A little at a time.

People who are millionaires—how did they get there? A little at a time.

How about people declaring bankruptcy? How did that happen? A little at a time.

People who are in great shape and people who weigh five hundred pounds? Yep. A little at a time.

Every day you make little decisions, and these little decisions are mounting up. What you do every day is turning you into the person you will become and leading you into the life you will live. It doesn't "just happen." You are *very* unlikely to win the lottery, meet Prince Charming while you are sleeping, or inherit a Fortune

500 company that makes you a CEO overnight. No, real life happens a little at a time.

Two Powerful Factors

Two impactful factors are always at play, but we often ignore them. One is called the "cumulative effect." This is the powerful effect produced by something happening, time and time again, over a long period of time.

The second factor is "compounding interest." Typically used in reference to finances, compounding interest speaks of the interest you get on interest. So, financially, you make an investment. That investment gains interest. You leave the interest in (thus "reinvesting the interest") and so the interest in the next period is earned on the amount you initially put in *and* the interest you have already accumulated. A wise man once said, "The most powerful force in the universe is compound interest."

This all may sound a little boring, but grasping the significance of these principles will completely change your life, because these principles are already shaping your life. If you look at your life you will realize that who you are—your relationships, finances, health, spiritual life—is impacted by, and even created by, the cumulative effect and compounding interest.

Financially

If a forty-year-old wants to have $1,000,000 in savings at age sixty-five, he has to invest $20 a day, every day. That's $7,300 invested every year.

If a twenty-year-old wants to have $1,000,000 in savings at age sixty-five, she only has to invest $2 a day. That's barely over $700 a year!

The inverse is true as well. How do you get $50,000 into consumer debt? Slowly. I know a guy who had $10,000 in Taco Bell debt. I'm not kidding. He put Taco Bell on his credit card every day. He went bankrupt one chalupa at a time.

Physically

Have you ever had a hundred-calorie snack pack? The problem you discover when you open a hundred-calorie bag is that there is virtually nothing in the bag! Get a hundred-calorie bag of Oreo Thins and you'll learn that they are not really Oreos; they are *very* thin, and there are *very* few of them in the bag.

So, check this out: you have an amount of calories you burn every day. If you eat one hundred fewer calories than you burn every day, you will lose ten pounds in a year. If you eat a hundred more calories than you burn, you will gain ten pounds a year. That's a twenty-pound difference, and one hundred calories is virtually nothing! But that small difference each day *will* add up.

Spiritually

It is harder to see, but these principles also apply spiritually. C. S. Lewis, a brilliant Christian thinker, wrote about this in his book *Mere Christianity*:

Good and evil both increase at compound interest. That is why the little decisions you and I make every day are of such infinite importance. The smallest good act today is the capture of a strategic point from which, a few months later, you may be able to go on to victories you never dreamed of. And apparently trivial indulgence in lust or anger today is the loss of a ridge, a railway line or bridgehead from which the enemy may launch an attack otherwise impossible.[1]

Do you get that? When we refuse God, when we sin, we think of it as an isolated incident. It's not. That little decision to sin is of "infinite importance." That one choice gives the devil a foothold to enter and work in our lives (see Eph. 4:27) and has the effect of hardening our hearts toward God (see Heb. 3:7–12). When we listen to God, when we submit to and obey him, it may seem like an isolated decision. It's not. That one act of obedience proves us trustworthy, trains us in faithfulness, and softens our hearts to continue to say yes to God (see Ezek. 11:19–20; 36:26–27).

Everything Matters

There was a book some years ago that encouraged people to not sweat "the small stuff" and to realize that "it's all small stuff." That may be true in reference to worrying, but there is no such thing as small stuff when it comes to our decisions. Because of the cumulative effect and compounding interest, eating that little hundred-calorie bag is not small stuff. Deciding to skip working out today is not small stuff. Telling your spouse "I love you" again is not small stuff. Having one more drink because everyone else is doing it is not small stuff.

Every day you make little decisions, and those little decisions are mounting up. What you do every day is turning you into the person you will become and leading you into the life you will live.

PONDER

What is something you don't currently like about your life? Your financial situation? Group of friends? Physical condition? Prayer life? Can you see how it has come about through a long series of small decisions?

PRACTICE

Decide, right now, on a small thing you will start doing right every day, starting today. It might be putting $5 a day into a savings account or index fund. Or having 5 minutes of "couch time" with your spouse (if you're married!) where you talk through your days. Or eating a hundred calories less a day than you have been.

PRAY

God, I know I will reap what I sow, but sometimes it's hard to remember that the seemingly insignificant decisions I make are actually significant. Please help me to remember that everything matters. Help me to always say yes to you.

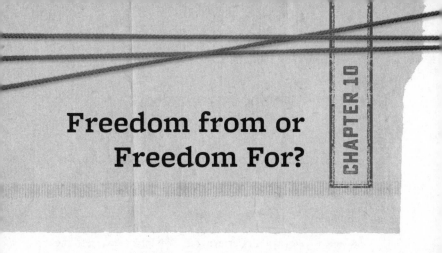

Freedom from or Freedom For?

CHAPTER 10

To the Jews who had believed him, Jesus said, "If you hold to my teaching, you are really my disciples. Then you will know the truth, and the truth will set you free." They answered him, "We are Abraham's descendants and have never been slaves of anyone. How can you say that we shall be set free?" Jesus replied, "Very truly I tell you, everyone who sins is a slave to sin. Now a slave has no permanent place in the family, but a son belongs to it forever. So if the Son sets you free, you will be free indeed." –John 8:31–36

I have always hated rules. If there was a rule, I wanted to break it. I wanted to be free.

I hate rules in general, and there are some that seem pointless. In fact, there are some laws in our country that are so dumb it's hard to believe they actually exist.

- In Oklahoma it's illegal to have a sleeping donkey in your bathtub after 7:00 p.m.

- In Alabama it's illegal to wear a fake moustache in church.
- In Zion, Illinois, it's illegal to give a cat or dog a lighted cigar.
- In Baltimore, Maryland, it's illegal to take a lion to the movies.

Growing Up

As kids, we all dream of growing up. We look forward to the day we can move out and finally be on our own. But why is that? It's not like being a kid is so tough. Kids generally don't have to pay rent or have very many responsibilities. When you think about it, being a kid is a pretty good gig.

But there's one big reason, I think, why kids look forward to being adults.

Freedom.

Freedom from all of those rules. Freedom to finally be in charge of your life. No longer under anyone's authority, able to make your own rules.

That's a good thing—but it can be a bad thing.

What Kind of Freedom?

We all want to be free. And, to be clear, if you are a Christian, the Bible definitely teaches that you are free. Christianity is *not* a set of rules, and God is not out to restrict your freedom. In fact, when God had the world just the way he wanted it, there was only one rule. God told Adam and Eve they were free to enjoy the perfect paradise he'd put them in. The only restriction was to not eat the fruit of one tree.

Later, Jesus arrived and said he came to "proclaim freedom for the prisoners" (Luke 4:18). He also said, "If the Son sets you free, you will be free indeed" (John 8:36). We're told, "It is for freedom that Christ has set us free" (Gal. 5:1).

God wants you to live free, but what does that mean? What kind of freedom is it?

It's *not* a freedom from God and his authority. In fact, we *can't* be free apart from God.

Think of a goldfish that wants to be free. For a fish to be free, it must be confined to water. If a fish breaks free from water, it dies. It's only by being confined to—connected to—water that it can be free.

One time I took my daughter to the pet store. She has the gift of empathy and felt so bad that each fish had to be confined to its bowl. She wanted to take it out, carry it around, keep it in her pocket. She wanted the fish to be free, but the freedom the fish needed was the freedom of life in the water.

In the same way, we were never meant to be free *from* God. It's only when we are connected to God, living under his authority, that we can truly be free.

We can see the reality of this with an addict. The addict breaks "free" from living under God's authority to indulge in some prohibited behavior—like drugs or pornography. But what happens? He *loses* his freedom as he's now unable to escape the compulsion to continue doing this thing he doesn't want to do. He didn't gain freedom. By breaking free from God, he *lost* his freedom.

God wants us to live free, but it's not a freedom *from*, it's a freedom *for*. We're free for God, free for love, free for living the life we were meant to live and truly want to live. We're free for a life of purpose and meaning, a life without regret or shame.

Isn't that the kind of life you want? Jesus came to set you free so you could live it. You're not free from, you're free for.

PONDER

What do you think Jesus meant when he said that he and his truth give us freedom? Have you experienced that yet? How so?

PRACTICE

Identify something that has you enslaved and remove your access to it. Today.

PRAY

God, you made me for freedom. Not freedom from you, but freedom for you and the life you created me to live. I repent of trying to rebel against your authority in my life. I want to live free, but I know I can only experience freedom if Jesus sets me free and if I live life in your truth. Help me to really live that way.

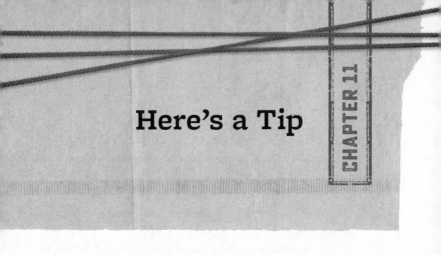

Here's a Tip

Now he who supplies seed to the sower and bread for food will also supply and increase your store of seed and will enlarge the harvest of your righteousness. You will be enriched in every way so that you can be generous on every occasion, and through us your generosity will result in thanksgiving to God. This service that you perform is not only supplying the needs of the Lord's people but is also overflowing in many expressions of thanks to God.
–2 Corinthians 9:10–12

You were made to make a difference. God gives you resources—time, talent, and treasure—to make a difference.

Do you think of money that way? Most don't. We think of money as a way to measure success, pay our bills, buy stuff we want, or create security. That's not what the Bible teaches about money. Jesus talked about money more than any other topic. Money is a big deal. It causes more problems for more people than just about anything else, and God wants us to understand it.

The Bible Teaches Us That . . .

Money is a test. Not a test as in something God puts in our way to trip us up, but a litmus test that reveals the true condition of our hearts. Jesus said, "No one can serve two masters. Either you will hate the one and love the other, or you will be devoted to the one and despise the other. You cannot serve both God and money" (Luke 16:13), and "For where your treasure is, there your heart will be also" (Matt. 6:21).

Your money is not yours. Your money is actually God's. I'm not saying you haven't worked for whatever money you have. Yes, you did earn it. But my question would be, How are you able to earn that money? Who gave you the ability to work? God did. God gave you your ability to earn money, he gave you money, and he's trusting you to steward it for him.

We are to be generous. "You will be enriched in every way so that you can be generous on every occasion" (2 Cor. 9:11). God gives us money so we can share it and make a difference.

Getting money can't make us happy; *giving* money can make us happy. Research actually backs this up, showing that people are happier when they give money away versus spending it on themselves.[1] Want to be happy? Be a cheerful giver (see 2 Cor. 9:7).

Waffle House

I was asked to speak in Orlando and was able to bring one of my three kids with me. I, of course, chose the one I love the most. (Kidding!) I brought my middle daughter, Finley, because we hadn't been spending a lot of time together lately. After my speaking engagement we were able to spend an awesome day at Disney World.

After Disney I told my daughter, "We can eat dinner at any restaurant you want." A few minutes later we drove past an expensive fine dining establishment . . . a Waffle House. My daughter saw the sign and exclaimed, "Daddy, can we go there? The sign says waffles!"

As we ate our waffles, we asked our waitress some questions. She shared her story. She was struggling. We encouraged her and prayed for her.

Finally, she dropped off the check. It was for like $11.37.

Finley and I walked up to the register to pay. I asked her, "Do you want to have some fun?"

She looked excited. "Are we going back to Disney?"

"No." I held up the check. "Let's give our waitress a $100 tip!"

Finley agreed, so we left the $100 tip and walked out. My daughter looked back through the glass front of the Waffle House. She happened to see our waitress at the moment she discovered our tip. Finley shouted, "Oh, Daddy, you should have seen her face! You should have seen her face!" Over and over she acted out how our waitress had reacted.

The next day we got home, and Finley's mother and siblings ambushed her with questions. "Finley, how was Disney?! Did you go to Animal Kingdom? Did you do the new *Avatar* ride? What was your favorite part?"

Finley's answer?

"Guys, you should have seen this lady's face."

PONDER

Is how you think about money the same as how God thinks about money?

PRACTICE

Choose a way you will increase your generosity.

PRAY

Father God, thank you for trusting me with your money. Help me to be a good steward of it. I know you gave it to me so I could give it away. I want to make a difference with my life and with the resources you've given me.

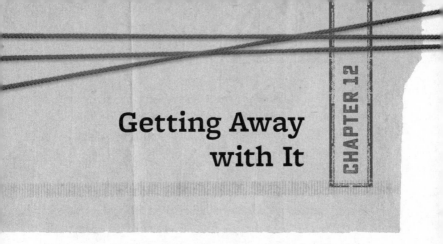

CHAPTER 12

Getting Away with It

There is nothing concealed that will not be disclosed, or hidden that will not be made known. What you have said in the dark will be heard in the daylight, and what you have whispered in the ear in the inner rooms will be proclaimed from the roofs. I tell you, my friends, do not be afraid of those who kill the body and after that can do no more. But I will show you whom you should fear: Fear him who, after your body has been killed, has authority to throw you into hell. Yes, I tell you, fear him.
–Luke 12:2–5

Does the thought of consequences scare you?

On the day of my wedding, my wife looked beautiful in her white dress. The preacher said great things about God and marriage and us. Finally, he told me, "You may kiss your bride," and I did.

After the ceremony, my new bride and I went to the foyer of the church and prayed. I thanked God for allowing me to escape the consequences of my sin. I had no STDs, no unwanted children, no psycho ex-girlfriend waiting to kill me after the ceremony. I had a past full of sexual sin, but I'd managed to get away with it.

Or so I thought.

Our first year of marriage, the "honeymoon period," was bliss.

In year two, we went from honeymoon to horrible. Turns out the consequences I thought I had avoided had been waiting, and they ambushed me. It was worse than an STD, illegitimate child, or psycho ex. I felt stuck in a marriage with a woman I had no idea how to love. After years of being enslaved to pornography, I had fed an addiction to variety, so monogamy seemed impossible. I felt trapped.

I didn't get away with it. The truth is, *no one* escapes the consequences of sin. You can escape the ultimate eternal punishment for your sins if you put your faith in Jesus and what he did on the cross, but you *cannot* escape the consequences of your sin. There's an ominous promise in the Bible that when you sin "you will be sinning against the LORD; and you may be sure that your sin will find you out" (Num. 32:23).

When we sin, we are on the road to suffering the consequences of our sin. And, honestly, that road trip isn't a fun one, even before we get to the unwanted destination.

The Consequences of Sin

I read a story by a man who had been struggling with a sin he refused to acknowledge. He would rationalize his sin, just like we all do. He felt like he had the sin "contained" within certain acceptable limits. He did feel guilty after doing it, and he thought that was the consequence of his sin.

He had to go to a conference and took some vacation time to drive up the New England coast. It was his favorite place in the world. Driving up the coast was always inspiring. In fact, the drive was the one thing that brought him far more joy than his pet sin.

But on this particular trip, he was shocked to discover that was no longer the case. He did all the things he loved to do—he stayed in homey inns with big fireplaces, ate by the waterfront, watched sailboats bobbing in the shimmering sea, took long walks along the beach, stopped at roadside stands for fresh lobster and crab. But this time he felt no pleasure. His emotional reaction was the same as if he was sitting at home, yawning, with nothing to do.

He finally realized his sin was deceiving him into thinking he was living life "to the fullest." The truth was, it was robbing him of life.

Unconfessed, ongoing sin turns family into an obligation, relationships into burdensome commitments, and what should be fun conversations into empty laughter. It will turn your career into a job, memories into blurry visions, and beautiful, meaningful moments into vacant ones.

Not only does sin empty life of fulfillment but it also leads to more sin. That's what we learn in Romans 1:18–31. If sin were truly just a guilty pleasure, more sin would mean more fun. But, no, God says the punishment for sin is sin. Our lives become increasingly empty, we are increasingly distant from God, and the end is death.

Take an honest look at your life. You may think you are getting away with it, but has sin left you hard and cold? Do you struggle to find joy in your relationship with God, your friends, or your church?

That repeated sin you enjoy? It's actually robbing you of life. You are *not* avoiding the consequences, you are *living* the consequences. And what's waiting at the end of the road you're on is worse.

What Do You Do with Your Sin?

Did you see the story in the news, back in 2013, when all six thousand garbage collectors in Madrid, Spain, went on strike? After just eight days, the city was overrun with trash. Garbage was literally filling the streets.

I think the same happens inside of us when we have sin we haven't dealt with. If we don't get rid of the sin, our soul will become overrun by it.

It's time to acknowledge your sin and confess it. There is something powerful about admitting your sin and saying it out loud.

When we confess our sin to God, he has compassion on us and we put ourselves in a position to prosper. "Whoever conceals their sins does not prosper, but the one who confesses and renounces them finds mercy" (Prov. 28:13).

When we confess to God, he forgives us and we put ourselves in position to be purified from our sins. "If we confess our sins, he is faithful and just and will forgive us our sins and purify us from all unrighteousness" (1 John 1:9).

When we confess our sins to some trusted friends, we put ourselves in position to be healed. "Therefore confess your sins to each other and pray for each other so that you may be healed. The prayer of a righteous person is powerful and effective" (James 5:16).

We confess and we repent. As we learned earlier, to *repent* means to turn around. We have been on a path of recurring sin, a path to suffering that leads to unwanted consequences. Repenting means to choose to reverse our direction. We commit, with God's help and the support and accountability of believing friends, to put our sin behind us and move in the direction of the life we've always wanted.

PONDER

What is a sin you think you're getting away with? How is that sin actually impacting your life right now? What consequences can you see coming?

PRACTICE

In chapter 2 you were asked to confess a hidden sin to God and to a trusted friend. Did you do it? If not, today is the day. Take that step onto the path to freedom. If you did confess but have another secret sin, confess that one today.

PRAY

God, I know my sin will find me out. The irony is that I sin because I'm selfish, but if I was *truly* selfish and did what was best for myself, I wouldn't sin. I confess my sin to you. Thank you for loving me and offering to purify me. Please do that in my life.

The Power of Habits

That, however, is not the way of life you learned when you heard about Christ and were taught in him in accordance with the truth that is in Jesus. You were taught, with regard to your former way of life, to put off your old self, which is being corrupted by its deceitful desires; to be made new in the attitude of your minds; and to put on the new self, created to be like God in true righteousness and holiness. –Ephesians 4:20–24

When Louie Vito was a kid, he made a sign and put it on the ceiling above his bed. The words he read every night as he was falling asleep said, "I am going to be a pro snowboarder."

Today, Louie Vito is . . . a pro snowboarder.

We love that story because it's about a guy who had a dream and accomplished it. *We* have dreams and want to accomplish them. In fact, you may be thinking about grabbing a marker and putting your dream on a piece of paper to hang above your bed.

That would not be a bad idea, but here's the thing: to make the dream happen, you have to get out of bed and do something about it.

An Ameritrade commercial showed Louie Vito winning a gold medal after an epic snowboarding run on a half-pipe. The commercial then starts going in reverse. We see Louie winning his first awards in his early teens. Then we watch Louie as a pre-teen practicing over and over in his front yard. Next, we see Louie's first times on a snowboard, then getting his first snowboard as a gift when he was a toddler. The idea is obvious: Louie didn't win gold just because he wanted to be a champion; he won gold because he *trained* to be a champion. No wonder he won gold; he started practicing when he was two years old and never stopped! The commercial ends with a text screen proclaiming, "Behind every big moment, there are lots of small ones," and a narrator telling us that we achieve our goals one small step at a time.

What You Repeatedly Do

What do you want to be a champion in? Do you want to be amazing at living for God? Being a spouse? Having an incredible career? Being a parent? Making a difference in the world?

Whatever it is, you are already in training. In fact, you trained yourself to succeed at your goal—or to fail at it—yesterday. And the day before. And all the days before that. Whether you realized it or not.

A wise man once said, "We are what we repeatedly do. Excellence, then, is not an act, but a habit." You are not going to become what you *want* to become. You are going to become what your habits lead you to become.

In Ephesians 4 and Colossians 3, we read about "putting off" our old self, our former practices and habits, and "putting on" our new self, our new practices and habits, so we can become who God made us to be.

It is all about habits, and this may mean you need to change some of yours.

Changing a Habit

In his book *The Power of Habit*, Charles Duhigg breaks a habit down into three connected pieces: a cue, a routine, and a reward.[1] Something happens (I feel lonely) that triggers me, I have a routine reaction to that cue (I look at porn, eat a tub of ice cream, or buy things I can't afford on the internet), and I receive a reward (I am able to ignore feeling lonely and instead I actually feel good—for a moment—because of the shot of dopamine my brain releases when I do my routine).

Duhigg says the way to change a habit is to break it into those three components and rewrite the routine we fall into when the cue happens, making sure the new routine also has a reward we will want.

In his book *Atomic Habits*, James Clear presents a similar way of thinking about habits, with one important addition.[2] He explains that our habits generally flow out of our identity. What you think about you is why you do what you do. As the Bible says, "For as he thinks in his heart, so is he" (Prov. 23:7 NKJV). So, if you want to change your habits, you first need to identify and change the self-thinking that is driving them.

You *can* change your habits and, if you do, you *will* change your life.

I will warn you: the first time, probably the first hundred times, it will feel awkward. You will want to respond to the old cue in the old way. Choosing to remember who you truly are and to do your new healthy routine will have to be a very conscious decision. But the good news is, eventually it won't feel so uncomfortable. In fact, after a while, your new habit will feel normal. It will actually become difficult to *not* do what right now might be very difficult to do.

I experienced this not long ago. Our family is a dessert family. (Ice cream is one of four food groups. Candy is my favorite meal.) Then I found out I have prediabetes, and that people die from diabetes. I decided to basically eliminate sugar from my diet for a year. At first, the cravings were unbearable. I couldn't sleep at night. But, as time passed, Snickers bars stopped haunting my dreams. In fact, when the year ended, I didn't really want candy or ice cream. *Not* eating sweets had become normal.

If I can eliminate sugar from my diet, you can do *anything*. You can change your habits and, if you do, you will change your life.

PONDER

Oswald Chambers wrote, "Routine is God's way of saving us between our times of inspiration."[3] What habits do you have that keep you connected to God and help you to grow in him?

PRACTICE

What habit do you need to build into your life? Decide to start it today. Ask a trusted friend to keep you accountable.

PRAY

God, to some extent I am what I repeatedly do. Help me to do the right thing every day so that I am becoming who you want me to be and living the life you want me to live.

CHAPTER 14

A Day of Rest

You are my hiding place; you will protect me from trouble and surround me with songs of deliverance. –Psalm 32:7

Today is a seventh day, so it's a day of rest from reading.

David wrote in Psalm 32:11, "Rejoice in the LORD and be glad, you righteous; sing, all you who are upright in heart!"

Why don't you take a couple minutes to sing your favorite worship song to God? Don't worry how you sound. He'll love it.

CHAPTER 15

The Lonely Generation

All the believers were together and had everything in common. They sold property and possessions to give to anyone who had need. Every day they continued to meet together in the temple courts. They broke bread in their homes and ate together with glad and sincere hearts, praising God and enjoying the favor of all the people. And the Lord added to their number daily those who were being saved. –Acts 2:44–47

Back in the very beginning, recorded for us in the first chapters of the first book of the Bible, God was creating the world, and he was on a roll.

He created the heavens and the earth and he said, "This is good!"

He created the water and the land and said, "This is good!"

He created the animals and birds and said, "This is good!"

He created chocolate Blue Bell ice cream and said, "This is good!"

71

But then he reached the pinnacle of his creative genius; he created a man, and for the first time God paused and said, "There's something *not* good here." The problem was that this first man was alone. God saw that it was not good, so he created a companion for the man, a woman, and said, "Now *that's* good."

What's fascinating is that this first man had great food, satisfying work, and a perfect relationship with God, and yet God evaluated his situation as being not good. Why? Because the one thing the man did not have was an answer for human loneliness. *That* was the problem.

We are not supposed to do life alone.

The Lonely Generation

Today's young adults are the most "connected" generation in the history of the world. For instance, the average adult Facebook user has 338 friends on the social network, and young adults tend to have even more than that.[1] Beyond connecting on Facebook, we also have Snapchat, Instagram, Twitter, LinkedIn, and a host of others.

We are the most connected generation, but we also may be the loneliest. Many of today's young adults have no close relationships of any kind. The statistics back this up. According to a study conducted by Duke University and the University of Arizona:

- Between 1985 and 2004, the number of people saying there was no one with whom they discussed important matters nearly tripled.

- 24.6 percent of Americans reported that they had no confidants, even counting close family members.
- Another 19.6 percent said they had just one confidant.
- More than half, 53.4 percent, did not have any confidants outside their family.[2]

Other studies have shown that the loneliest people in society are young adults.[3] For example, one Australian study found that those ages twenty-four to thirty-four were by far the most likely to be lonely, with 30 percent saying they "frequently feel lonely." Among those ages thirty-five to thirty-nine, only 6 percent said they often felt lonely.[4]

How can we be the most connected generation *and* the loneliest? I believe our extreme connectedness is part of the reason we lack true connections. You can't have 338 close friends. It's impossible. But we think of these people as our friends, and it can keep us from developing true friendships. I wonder, How many people do you hang out with and discuss important life issues with on a daily or weekly basis?

Community

Repeatedly, research is proving what God told us all those years ago, "It is not good for the man to be alone" (Gen. 2:18), and that the best way to live is in community.

The Harvard Grant Study followed the lives of 268 physically and mentally healthy Harvard college sophomores from the classes of 1939–1944. The goal of this seventy-five-year study was to answer the question, Why are people who are happy and fulfilled happy and fulfilled? The answer? The heading of the study results announced, "Harvard study, almost eighty years old, has proved that embracing community helps us live longer and be happier." Turns out people with the strongest relational ties are the happiest people. One psychiatrist involved said, "Connection is the whole shooting match."[5]

Another research project studied people for years, seeking to solve the riddle, Why are the people who are the most satisfied and emotionally well adjusted the most satisfied and emotionally well adjusted? The result, published in an article called "Why Our Mental Health Takes a Village,"[6] is that they have a great group of friends. Interestingly, it wasn't people who had *one* best friend, or a great marriage with a supportive spouse, but those who had a great *group* of friends.

Throughout the Bible, God calls us to live in community. Looks like he knew what he was talking about.

If you are not living in community, you need to. If you don't know where to find it, I would encourage you to get into a small group at your church. The people in it won't be perfect, but neither are you. I've found that when imperfect people commit to living in community, in Jesus's name, great things happen. You will live longer and be happier, more satisfied, and more emotionally well adjusted. More importantly, you will be living life the way God designed you to.

PONDER

Do you have anyone you are close enough to that it wouldn't be weird if you just dropped by their place?

PRACTICE

If you are not in a small group, take a step to get into one today. If you *are* in a small group, take a step to grow your relationship with at least one of the people in it today.

PRAY

God, you said it is not good for us to be alone, and I do not want to live that way. Help me to find and live in true community that reflects who you are and who you have designed me to be.

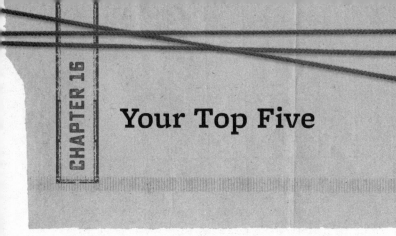

CHAPTER 16

Your Top Five

Bad company corrupts good character. –1 Corinthians 15:33

Motivational speaker Jim Rohn is widely attributed as saying, "You are the average of the five people you spend the most time with." Yikes! If the people we hang out with have that much influence on who we are, we'd better choose some good friends!

Here's another quote I've heard people say that makes a lot of sense to me: "Show me your friends and I'll show you your future." More yikes! If the people we hang out with have that much influence on who we'll become, we'd better choose some good friends!

I've experienced the truth of these statements. In middle school I had four friends I spent all my free time with, and we definitely influenced each other's behavior. Our favorite activity was to TP the houses of girls we liked. If someone drove by while we were wrapping the house in toilet paper, we would all drop our pants and moon them. Yes, we were a mature group.

In college I had another "band of brothers" like that. We partied together and got in fights together.

Your Top Five

As you might guess, I wasn't interested in following Jesus back then, but I am today. Since you're reading this book, I assume you are too. Actually, I'm not just interested in following Jesus; it's the passion of my life. I hope it's yours too.

When we think about what will help or hinder us in really following Jesus, I wonder if we realize how influential a factor our friends are. Think back to that "five people you spend the most time with" quote. Isn't it true that . . .

- if your top five exercise a lot, you'll be more likely to exercise?
- if your top five party a lot, you'll be more likely to party?
- if your top five read the Bible every day, you'll be more likely to read the Bible?
- if your top five gossip, you'll be more likely to gossip?

Here's how the Bible says it: "Walk with the wise and become wise, for a companion of fools suffers harm" (Prov. 13:20).

What's interesting is that Solomon wrote that proverb. Solomon became a king at a young age. God told Solomon he could ask for anything, and Solomon chose wisdom. He became incredibly wise and wrote the Proverbs. His life got off to a great start, but

Solomon didn't obey God or even listen to his own wisdom. Here's what happened:

> King Solomon, however, loved many foreign women besides Pharaoh's daughter—Moabites, Ammonites, Edomites, Sidonians and Hittites. They were from nations about which the LORD had told the Israelites, "You must not intermarry with them, because they will surely turn your hearts after their gods." Nevertheless, Solomon held fast to them in love. He had seven hundred wives of royal birth and three hundred concubines, and his wives led him astray. As Solomon grew old, his wives turned his heart after other gods, and his heart was not fully devoted to the LORD his God, as the heart of David his father had been. (1 Kings 11:1–4)

What happened? I guess we could say, to Solomon, "Show me your wives and I'll show you your future." Solomon married women who didn't share his faith in God, and soon he shared their lack of faith in God. Solomon became more and more like the people he spent the most time with.

The same is true for you and me. We need to be careful to not live like Solomon lived but to live by what he said, "Walk with the wise and become wise, for a companion of fools suffers harm" (Prov. 13:20).

PONDER

Who do you spend the most time with? How are they influencing you?

PRACTICE

If you realize that you don't have a "top five" who are influencing you in a positive way, choose to spend more time with some different friends. Getting more involved at your church (by joining a group or team) is probably a great way to find some new friends.

PRAY

God, I realize that a big part of what makes me who I am today and will determine my future are the people I spend the most time with. Please give me friends who are faith-filled followers of Jesus and can help me to better follow Jesus and live the life you have for me.

CHAPTER 17

Can't We All Just Get Along?

If your brother or sister sins, go and point out their fault, just between the two of you. If they listen to you, you have won them over. But if they will not listen, take one or two others along, so that "every matter may be established by the testimony of two or three witnesses." If they still refuse to listen, tell it to the church; and if they refuse to listen even to the church, treat them as you would a pagan or a tax collector. –Matthew 18:15–17

One of the cool things about you is that you are unique. One of the annoying things about everyone else is that they are not like you. That's why you feel normal and everyone else seems . . . weird. Because we're all unique.

Do you know what happens if you take two very different people and put them in a relationship? "You complete me"? No. *Conflict* happens.

You are not only unique but also selfish. So is everyone you are ever going to meet. Take two selfish people and put them in a relationship and, yep, conflict happens.

Conflict makes relationships hard, but relationships are incredibly important. If you want your relationships to be healthy and happy, you need to be great at resolving conflict. Before I finally learned how to handle conflict correctly, I unintentionally killed some relationships. I once paid for a best friend to go to a water park with me because he was broke. At the park he bought a puka shell necklace. *Wait, I thought he was broke!* I confronted him right there, yelling and shoving him backward. I "won" the argument but lost a friend.

So, how should we handle conflict? The Bible can teach us.

Step 1: Acknowledge and Ask Forgiveness for Your Role in the Problem

It is easy to assume the other person is at fault, but you need to take responsibility for your part of the problem. Jesus said, "How can you say to your brother, 'Brother, let me take the speck out of your eye,' when you yourself fail to see the plank in your own eye? You hypocrite, first take the plank out of your eye, and then you will see clearly to remove the speck from your brother's eye" (Luke 6:42). This is the right thing to do, and by taking responsibility for your part of the problem, you will help the other person do the same.

Step 2: Talk to the Person in Private

You're hurt. You recognize you played a part, and you're ready to acknowledge that and ask forgiveness. What do you do now? You go to the person. (Read that again: "You go to the person.")

You—not someone else.

Go to—not text or email.

The person—not to another person to gossip or complain, not to Facebook to air your grievance.

You go to the other person, not with the goal of winning but with the goal of a restored, healthy relationship.

Jesus was very clear about this. In Matthew 18, he said to go and talk to the person, one-on-one. Acknowledging and asking forgiveness for your part of the problem would probably be a great place to start. Then graciously explain how you feel that the person sinned against you. They may not realize they did anything wrong, so it's only fair to give them a chance to apologize and make it right.

If they admit they were wrong and ask for forgiveness, you forgive them. Your relationship is restored. You can celebrate by doing a Fortnite dance together or sharing a sharing-size bag of M&Ms. (Confession: I have *never* shared a sharing-size bag of M&Ms.)

If they *won't* acknowledge they have sinned against you, move on to step 3.

Step 3: Bring Others In

Jesus said, "But if they will not listen, take one or two others along, so that 'every matter may be established by the testimony of two or three witnesses.' If they still refuse to listen, tell it to the church; and if they refuse to listen even to the church, treat them as you would a pagan or a tax collector" (vv. 16–17).

If your first attempt didn't work, bring a friend or two with you to approach the other person again. Who should you bring? Either a witness to the wrong or someone the two of you are in community with.

If that doesn't work, bring in church leadership. Church leaders should be mature and have some experience in conflict resolution. Hopefully, they can help you move toward reconciliation.

If not, Jesus says to "treat them as you would a pagan (a nonbeliever) or a tax collector." What does that mean? Well, Jesus spent most of his time with pagans and tax collectors. So this does not mean you avoid them or treat them badly. I think it means you continue to love them and be friends with them, but you stop assuming they're following Jesus. You don't have an expectation they'll obey God. You look for opportunities to share the gospel with them. You may have to be careful to not put yourself in a position to be hurt by them again.

PONDER

What unresolved conflict do you have in your life?

PRACTICE

Is there a strained relationship where you've been avoiding conflict? Prayerfully go to that person, acknowledge your fault, and
graciously point out theirs.

PRAY

Lord, I know you live in relationship and you created me to live in
relationship. Relationships are so important but can be so hard.
Please help me to have healthy relationships and, when things go
wrong, to not avoid conflict or do it wrong but to handle conflict
the way Jesus taught us to.

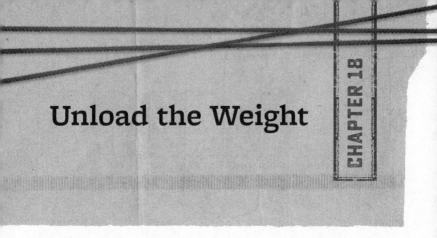

CHAPTER 18

Unload the Weight

Therefore, as God's chosen people, holy and dearly loved,
clothe yourselves with compassion, kindness, humility,
gentleness and patience. Bear with each other and forgive
one another if any of you has a grievance against someone.
Forgive as the Lord forgave you. And over all these virtues
put on love, which binds them all together in perfect unity.
–Colossians 3:12–14

I was leading a mission trip to Brazil. Our team would be staying
on a boat, which is cool but restricting when it comes to what
you can bring. I told our team they could each only bring a small
suitcase, and it had to weigh less than fifty pounds.

At the airport, everyone successfully checked in, until one member of my team walked up to the counter. She put her suitcase on
the scale, and it weighed over fifty pounds. I frowned, she apologized, and we unzipped her suitcase so we could find something
to put in someone else's luggage. Inside her suitcase was a bag of
rocks.

I turned to her, confused. "Why do you have a bag of rocks? You can't bring rocks to Brazil."

She looked a little embarrassed and told me, "I'm sorry, JP, but I have to. I'm in a Bible study about forgiveness. We're learning that unforgiveness is a weight we choose to carry. We all agreed to carry around a rock for each person we have bitterness toward. I have to carry these rocks until I forgive those people."

Forgive? Them?

We like the idea of forgiving—until we have to do the forgiving. Part of the reason we may be slow to forgive is because we have mistaken ideas. God tells us to forgive, but what exactly is he asking us to do?

Forgiveness is not saying what happened was not wrong. God tells us to forgive in Romans 12:17, saying, "Do not repay anyone evil for evil." Did you notice he called what happened to you "evil"? It *was* wrong, but we still need to forgive.

Forgiveness is *not* forgetting. We've all been told, "Forgive and forget," but we can't forget. Our minds don't work like that.

Forgiveness is *not* just saying the words, "I forgive you." Forgiving may include saying those words, but we can say those words and not really forgive.

Forgiveness is *not* pretending it didn't happen. Too often, our version of forgiving is really just burying our feelings. That never works.

Forgiveness *is* grace. Grace means to give someone the opposite of what they deserve.

Forgiveness *is* releasing our right to retaliate. Instead of seeking revenge, we give mercy. We know justice is God's job. We're told, in Romans 12:18–20,

> If it is possible, as far as it depends on you, live at peace with everyone. Do not take revenge, my dear friends, but leave room for God's wrath, for it is written: "It is mine to avenge; I will repay," says the Lord. On the contrary:
>
> > "If your enemy is hungry, feed him;
> >   if he is thirsty, give him something to drink.
> > In doing this, you will heap burning coals on his head."

Forgiving the person who hurt you might sound impossible but "with God all things are possible" (Matt. 19:26). God is not asking you to do this on your own. He set the example of forgiving someone who has sinned against you by forgiving *you*. And he offers to empower you to do what you cannot do on your own.

Forgive for You

You might be thinking that if you forgave those people, they wouldn't appreciate it or even care. But God doesn't ask you to forgive to heal the other person. He asks you to forgive to heal yourself. Not forgiving those people is not damaging them, it's damaging you.

I talk to so many young adults who feel stuck, unable to move into the future God has for them. They don't see why, but I do. They're still chained to their past because they still haven't forgiven.

They're weighed down by what has happened to them, and it's time to unload the weight.

That brings me back to our mission trip to Brazil. The young lady who brought the rocks spent the week experiencing God's grace in a powerful way. It helped her to better understand the grace God had given her through Christ. On the last day of the trip I found her on top of the boat we were staying in. She was throwing her rocks into the Amazon River, one by one. For each rock she threw, she shouted, "I forgive you! I forgive you!"

Her voice, and the rocks hitting the water, were the sound of freedom.

PONDER

Who have you not yet forgiven?

PRACTICE

Put a rock in a bag for each person you have not forgiven. Carry the bag until you forgive them.

PRAY

Father God, thank you for forgiving me through Jesus's death. Help me to forgive as you have forgiven me. I don't know if I can do it on my own, but I can do anything through you.

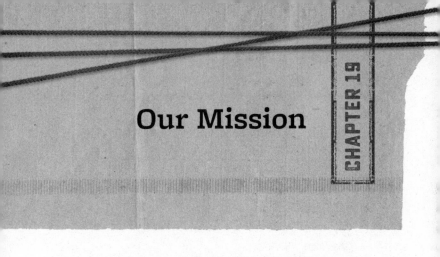

CHAPTER 19

Our Mission

Then Jesus came to them and said, "All authority in heaven and on earth has been given to me. Therefore go and make disciples of all nations, baptizing them in the name of the Father and of the Son and of the Holy Spirit, and teaching them to obey everything I have commanded you. And surely I am with you always, to the very end of the age."
–Matthew 28:18–20

At the gym I met a guy I'll call Pablo. We started talking, and eventually I asked him, "Between one and ten, how certain are you that you'll go to heaven?"

Pablo thought for a moment, then said, "Two."

I asked, "Why only a two?"

"Man." Pablo took a deep breath. "I've done some things."

I thought about the apostle Paul, who God sought though he had been involved in killing people. I asked Pablo, "How many people have you killed?" (Thinking he'd say none.)

I saw Pablo start counting on his fingers and thought, *Oh shoot! You* have *done some things!*

I interrupted Pablo's counting. "Do you think you have to go to hell to pay for the bad things you've done?"

Pablo nodded yes.

"What if I told you," I said as I looked right in Pablo's eyes, "that it's all already been paid for?"

"By who?" Pablo seemed confused.

"By Jesus."

After that conversation, I kind of thought I was the evangelism king. I told my wife how I was able to share the good news of Jesus with Pablo in such a clear, compelling way.

That's our mission in life: to share the good news of Jesus in a clear, compelling way.

It's also why I go to the gym.

The *second* reason is to work out and *attempt* to stay fit.

The *first* reason is to fulfill my mission in life.

The mission of everyone who is close to God is to help other people get close to God.

The mission of every follower of Jesus is to help other people to follow Jesus.

The mission of everyone going to heaven is to help everyone go to heaven.

Think about it: Why didn't God just bring you straight to heaven when you got saved? If we are going to heaven in the end, why did he leave us here to have to live our lives? It's because he has work for us to do, the "work of an evangelist" (see 2 Tim. 4:5). God saved you so he could use you to save others.

Jesus said he came to "seek and save the lost." We are Jesus's followers. We care about what Jesus cares about. We take his mission as our own.

To fulfill our mission, we need to see like Jesus saw and do what Jesus did.

See Like Jesus Saw

Jesus was traveling through some towns, and we're told,

> When he saw the crowds, he had compassion on them, because they were harassed and helpless, like sheep without a shepherd. Then he said to his disciples, "The harvest is plentiful but the workers are few. Ask the Lord of the harvest, therefore, to send out workers into his harvest field." (Matt. 9:36–38)

Jesus saw people who were harassed and helpless—no one seemed to care, give them attention, or try to help them. Jesus saw them as "sheep without a shepherd." The idea is that these were God's children, but they were doing life without their heavenly Father. They didn't have God in their lives. That's how Jesus saw them, and that is the worst sight in the world. We're told that Jesus "had compassion" on them. The word translated "had compassion" more literally means to have your intestines twisted. When Jesus saw people without God, his stomach hurt.

How do *you* see people? Do you view your waitress as a person who is there to serve you or as someone who either has or does not have God? Do you view your college friend as a person you have fun hanging out with or as someone who desperately needs Jesus? Do you view your boss as the person who signs your paychecks or as someone you could bring to heaven with you?

We are Jesus's followers when we see people the way Jesus saw them.

Do What Jesus Did

We need to see like Jesus saw and do what Jesus did. What did Jesus do? "For God so loved the world that he gave his one and only Son, that whoever believes in him shall not perish but have eternal life" (John 3:16). God sent Jesus to help people believe in him so they could have eternal life.

That was the mission God gave Jesus, and then Jesus gave it to us. He said, "As the Father has sent me, I am sending you" (John 20:21). He sent us to help people believe in him so they could have eternal life.

Jesus was willing to do whatever it took—including dying on a cross—to help people come into a relationship with God.

We are Jesus's followers, so we are willing to do whatever it takes.

If you made a list of all the lost people God has put in your life—friends, roommates, classmates, coworkers, neighbors, your boss, your garbage collector, your barista—and for each person made a list of what you have done to help them come into a relationship with God, what would you see? How many prayers have you prayed for them? How many spiritual conversations have you started? How have you served them? How many times have you invited them to church?

And, to be clear: with almost all of those things, once is not enough.

Pablo

Remember Pablo?

A week after telling him about Jesus, I saw Pablo at the gym again. I walked up and asked, with a smile, "Hey, Pablo. Between one and ten, how certain are you that you'll go to heaven?"

Pablo's response was quick. "Two."

Noooooooo! Apparently, I am not the evangelism king.

I asked, "Why a two, Pablo?"

"Man, I told you, I've done some things."

Realizing I needed help, I shot up a quick prayer, and then said, "Pablo, one time I got a haircut and paid my barber, then walked out of the barbershop. As I walked out, a guy from my church saw me. He went up to the cash register and told my barber he wanted to pay for my haircut. What do you think the barber told him?"

Pablo didn't hesitate. "He would have said it's already been paid for."

"That's right." I spoke slowly, hoping the words would sink in. "It was already paid for, and you cannot pay for something that's already been paid for. So, Pablo, why do you want to pay for your sins when they've already been paid for by Jesus?"

Pablo looked thoughtful. I kept going.

"If I gave you tickets for the Mavs game and you showed up for it tonight," I asked, "would they let you in?"

"Yes."

"Why would they let you in?"

"Because I have a ticket."

"That's right. And if they asked you if you paid for your ticket, you would tell them no, it was a gift. And they would let you in because that ticket was paid for. Pablo, there is going to come a day when you stand before God. The only reason he would allow you into heaven is if you've put your faith in Jesus, trusting he paid for your sins and gave you the gift of eternal life. You'll be able to say, 'I have a ticket, and it's been paid for.'"

When I saw Pablo again I asked a third time, "Between one and ten, how certain are you that you'll go to heaven?"

Pablo smiled and said, "I'm a ten . . . because God gave me a ticket in named Jesus. He died for my sins and rose from the dead. He paid my way in. I can't pay for something that's already been paid for."

That message is my mission. That's your mission too.

PONDER

Who has God put in your life who is far from him? How do you see that person?

PRACTICE

Set up a time to hang out with your friend who is far from God. During that time, start a spiritual conversation.

PRAY

God, you sent Jesus to the world to help people believe in him so they could go to be with you. Now you have sent me to the world to do the same. Please help me to see people the way Jesus did, and to join Jesus's mission of seeking and saving the lost.

CHAPTER 20

Time to Commit

> Commit your way to the LORD; trust in him and he will do this: He will make your righteous reward shine like the dawn, your vindication like the noonday sun. –Psalm 37:5–6

If you search the internet for "weird entries in the *Guinness Book of World Records*," you'll see incredible accomplishments achieved by extraordinary people, such as . . .

the largest gathering of people dressed as penguins: 373.

the most people head-banging simultaneously: 320.

the most naked riders on an amusement park ride: 102.

But the record I am interested in was set by a guy named Octavio Guillen. He asked a lady named Adriana Martinez to marry him in 1902. But he wasn't sure. He kept putting it off. Finally, they got married . . . in 1969. It is the longest engagement ever: sixty-seven years![1]

Octavio may have set the record, and it may have happened before most of us were born, but that fear of commitment—not just in dating—is alive and well today. In fact, sometimes I think it is one of the defining characteristics of my generation.

The problem is that refusing to commit messes things up.

Hot Mess

I like to paint. One time I was painting a guy in a boat, but I thought better of it and turned what I had started into a tree in a field. Unfortunately, the tree in the field was not turning out the way I hoped either, so I pivoted. I made the field into a lake, turned the tree that had been a boat back into a boat, and turned the blue afternoon sky into a starry night. Want to know how the painting ended up? It was a mess. One big, sloppy, hot mess.

I have seen countless young adults who went from one boyfriend or girlfriend to another, from in college to out of college to in college to out of college, from majoring in English Lit to Economics to Theater to Sociology, from working as a teacher to a waitress to a receptionist to a personal trainer, from church to church to church, from living with one set of friends to another to another—and it all becomes a big, sloppy, hot mess.

I remember when FOMO was a term only young, hip people used; it's now in the Oxford Dictionary. Fear of missing out is increasingly pervasive, and it's increasingly keeping us from committing and causing us to duck out on our commitments.

The thing is, followers of Jesus should not fear missing out on the latest movie, hippest trend, hottest party, coolest restaurant, biggest game, better bae, or more exotic vacation. Followers of Jesus only fear missing out on his will for their lives.

Not struggling with FOMO means Jesus's followers can live in peace and with a quiet confidence. Not struggling with FOMO allows Jesus's followers to commit. They make and keep commitments. They are fully present and fully loyal to the relationships they are in, the employer they have, and the church they are a part of.

I see a lack of commitment in all arenas of life, but one that really concerns me is when young people don't commit to a church.

The Church Buffet

Ever been to a buffet in Las Vegas? While I was writing this book I had to go to Vegas, and I had lunch at the buffet at Caesar's. The options were overwhelming. Shrimp. Crab legs. Brisket. (Brisket that would even pass the test for us Texans.) There were incredible Asian and Italian and Mexican sections. Don't even get me started on the desserts. There was an entire buffet of desserts. I got six of them.

That is fine for lunch, but too often we can approach church that way. We have a consumer mindset, asking, What can I get out of this? We take a little from this church because it has good preaching. We go to a different church because it has better worship. We go to another church for their singles ministry.

The problem is that church is not meant to be a buffet you go to. In fact, church really isn't something you go to at all. It is something you *are*.

Church is family, and you are called to be a part of *one*. Can you imagine choosing one family to have breakfast with because they have Cinnamon Toast Crunch, then picking a different family to eat dinner with because the mom is a great cook? Going to watch TV at night with another family because they like to binge-watch the same Netflix shows as you, then spending weekends with yet another family because they have a little more money and go on some cool road trips? The idea is absurd. There is no such thing as a family-shopper or a family-hopper, but there are lots of church-shoppers and church-hoppers. We should consider that absurd too.

You need to commit to *one* church. One church where you are known, serve, find community, are held accountable, submit to the elders, and contribute your time, talent, and treasure.

My story is that I went to church, week after week, but my life never changed. I was going to church but I was not committed. I ignored the flyers for newcomer classes and, on my way out, would bump my head against the "Get Connected Here" sign.

The day I decided to commit—not only to God but also to a church—was the day my life started to change.

Commitment Leads to Greatness

It's not just true of church. Anything great comes through commitment. People who fear missing out and jump around don't become great at anything. They struggle in school, in their careers, in their relationships.

So, "Commit to the LORD whatever you do, and he will establish your plans" (Prov. 16:3).

PONDER

Where does FOMO plague your life? What do you think is really at the heart of your fear?

PRACTICE

Is there someone you have broken a commitment with, and you need to apologize to them? Why don't you do that today?

PRAY

God, I want to be someone who makes and keeps commitments. I commit to you what I do. Please help me and establish my plans.

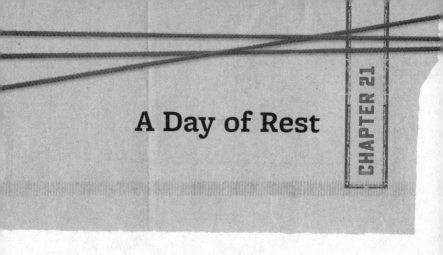

CHAPTER 21

A Day of Rest

And let us consider how we may spur one another on toward love and good deeds, not giving up meeting together, as some are in the habit of doing, but encouraging one another—and all the more as you see the Day approaching. –Hebrews 10:24–25

No reading today!

We learned this week about the importance of our relationships. Why not get ahold of some friends you have community with and ask them to get together today?

CHAPTER 22

Clearness Committee

Therefore, I urge you, brothers and sisters, in view of God's mercy, to offer your bodies as a living sacrifice, holy and pleasing to God—this is your true and proper worship. Do not conform to the pattern of this world, but be transformed by the renewing of your mind. Then you will be able to test and approve what God's will is—his good, pleasing and perfect will. For by the grace given me I say to every one of you: Do not think of yourself more highly than you ought, but rather think of yourself with sober judgment, in accordance with the faith God has distributed to each of you. For just as each of us has one body with many members, and these members do not all have the same function, so in Christ we, though many, form one body, and each member belongs to all the others. We have different gifts, according to the grace given to each of us. –Romans 12:1–6

There is something Quakers do that I think you should do.

I'm not asking you to become a Quaker. Quakers are a Christian denomination started in the 1600s, but, again, I am not asking you to join them. I'm simply suggesting you do one thing they do. I know, I know, you thought Quakers only do oatmeal. Yes, they do a good job with oatmeal, but they do a good job with something else too, and it has everything to do with . . . your job.

Regrets

Have you ever wondered what regrets you'll have later in life? Probably not, but it may not be a bad idea. If we predict some of our regrets now, we may be able to avoid experiencing them later.

Bronnie Ware is a nurse in Australia who cares for the dying as they live out the last weeks of their lives. Hearing the honest confessions of people on their deathbeds led her to write the book *The Top Five Regrets of the Dying*.[1] So, what has she found to be the most common regret people have at the end of their lives? "I wish I'd had the courage to live a life true to myself, not the life others expected of me."

Wow. That can be true in many ways. One that's especially common is with career choice. Studies conducted by Gallup reveal that 85 percent of Americans hate their jobs.[2]

Why? I think we listen to the wrong voices. It may be parents have a career they want us to pursue, or friends have expectations we want to meet, or the idea of success and financial rewards calls us.

Clearness Committee

In his book *Let Your Life Speak*, Parker Palmer wrote about discovering your unique calling from God. He pointed out that the word *vocation*, one of our words for a job, comes from the Latin word for *voice*. There used to be an idea that to discover your vocation required very careful listening to God's voice.

Palmer loved his work as a college professor but was offered the presidency of a university. It would have meant an increase in pay, status, and influence. From a career standpoint, it was a no-brainer. He was ready to say yes but couldn't, yet. He couldn't because he was . . . a Quaker. (You thought I forgot about the Quaker thing. Nope.) The Quakers have a tradition where, when faced with an important decision about calling, they gather a half-dozen friends together to serve as a "clearness committee." This group meets to ask questions to help the person discern God's voice more clearly.

The first questions the committee asked Palmer were easy. What would his vision be for this school? What mission would it serve in society? Then someone asked what seemed to be a simple question. "Parker, what would you like about being president?" This stopped Parker in his tracks. He had to think for quite a while. Finally, he said, "Well, I wouldn't like all the politics involved, I wouldn't like having to give up my study and teaching, I wouldn't like to have to raise funds . . ." The person who had asked the question interrupted. "Yes, but the question was what *would* you like?" Parker was frustrated. "I'm coming to that. I wouldn't like to have to give up my summer vacations, I wouldn't like . . ." The question was asked a third time. Palmer wrote,

> I felt compelled to give the only answer I possessed, an answer that came from the very bottom of my barrel, an answer that appalled even me as I spoke it. "Well," said I, in the smallest voice I possess, "I guess what I'd like most is getting my picture in the paper with the word 'President' under it." I was sitting with seasoned Quakers who knew that though my answer was laughable, my mortal soul was clearly at stake! They did not laugh at all but went into a long and serious silence—a silence in which I could only sweat and inwardly groan. Finally my questioner broke the silence with a question that cracked all of us up—and cracked me open: "Parker," he said, "can you think of an easier way to get your picture in the paper?"[3]

Palmer said no to the job offer. If he had taken the job, it would have led to frustration and fatigue. He might have blamed the university he was working for or the people he was working with, but the truth would have been that he was in the wrong job. Palmer writes, "You cannot choose your calling. You must let your life speak."[4]

How about you? Are you living a life that is true to yourself? Does your job fit you?

Vocation is not a career I pursue, it's a calling I listen for.

PONDER

Have you thought of your job more as a career or a calling? How did you include God in choosing your vocation?

PRACTICE

Why not put together a clearness committee of your own? Ask three to six friends (you may want to bribe them with pizza) to get together to ask you questions (not give you advice) to help you listen for God's voice in a decision (career or otherwise) that you have to make.

PRAY

God, thank you for creating me unique and for having a unique plan for my life. Please help me to listen to you and to listen to my life. I want to live out your good, pleasing, and perfect will. I surrender to you and to your leadership.

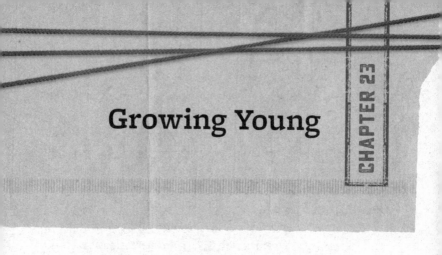

Growing Young

At that time the disciples came to Jesus and asked, "Who, then, is the greatest in the kingdom of heaven?" He called a little child to him, and placed the child among them. And he said: "Truly I tell you, unless you change and become like little children, you will never enter the kingdom of heaven." –Matthew 18:1–3

As a kid, what did you want to be when you grew up?

Do you remember the commercial from a few years ago where a kid stared into the camera and said, "Someday, I'd like to claw my way up to middle management"? Another kid said, "I want to have a brown nose."

It's funny because no kid is like that. I don't know what you wanted to be when you grew up, but I know the goal was not, "Pension plan, health benefits, forty-hour cap on my work week." No. Kids have great expectations, big dreams, a lust for life. Kids live with a sense of wonder.

Unfortunately, it's easy to lose that sparkle in our eye. Over time it can start to feel like nothing is that big of a deal.

I've talked to people who believe Jesus really was the Son of God, really died on the cross, and really rose from the dead—and their reaction is, "Ehhhh." Like, *Yeah, it's true, but it just doesn't seem like that big of a deal.* What?! People don't just go around rising from the dead. It *is* a big deal.

I know people who believe God answers prayer but rarely pray. Excuse me?! You have access to God. The supernatural creator of the universe listens to you and will respond to you, and you don't think it's worth taking some time to do that?

I know people who understand God has offered to partner with them in changing the world, but instead of engaging with that, they mostly watch TV or play video games. Really?!

I'm not sure what the problem is, but I wonder if it's apathy. We act like it's not a big deal, but it *is*. Do we need to recapture the great expectations, big dreams, and lust for life of our childhood? Perhaps what we need is a kid-like sense of wonder.

Like a Child

On several occasions Jesus told his followers he wanted them to become like children. It's fascinating to me that he said that, but no one asked him what he meant. You'd think someone would have asked, "Jesus, you're telling us to become like children. So . . . food fights? Making fart noises with our armpits? What are you looking for, here?" But no one did.

Jesus said we must become children, and I guess it's up to us to understand, maybe even guess at, what he meant. I can't say for sure, but I think part of it is overcoming apathy and regaining that sense of wonder.

Author G. K. Chesterton wrote about how as children grow up it takes more and more to evoke wonder in them.[1] He said you can illustrate this by thinking of reading the same story to three young children.

To a seven-year-old you dramatically read, "Little Tommy got up, walked to the door, and opened the door. And suddenly a dragon jumped in front of Tommy." The seven-year-old's eyes get wide and remain transfixed, until she's assured Tommy whipped the dragon.

Read the same part of that story to a four-year-old. "Little Tommy got up, walked to the door, and opened . . . the . . . door!" The four-year-old's eyes get big as she tingles with the anticipation of what might lie behind that door.

Start to read the same story to an eighteen-month-old. "Little Tommy got up and walked . . . to . . . the . . . door." The little guy's eyes are ready to explode. He's like, *Forget the door, this little Tommy can walk?! Wow!*

See what's happening? At age seven, you need a dragon to evoke wonder. At age four, the mere gesture of slowly opening a door strikes a chord. And for the eighteen-month-old, it's a pretty big deal to get up on two legs. As we grow older it takes more and more to evoke wonder.

I know we've all probably had a lot of people tell us to grow up, but maybe what we really need is to grow young. We need to overcome apathy and regain that sense of wonder.

PONDER

What about God and the life he has for you—have you been taking it for granted?

PRACTICE

Where in your life does it look like you don't believe or don't really care? A lack of prayer? Not sharing your faith? Not giving generously? What would your life look like if you overcame your apathy? Start living that way! Even if you don't "feel it," *choose* to start living that way.

PRAY

God, you are amazing! You have put me in an awe-inspiring world. You, incredibly, became a person so you could die for me and remove my sins. You offer to listen to me, answer my prayers, and partner with me in changing the world. Wow! Please don't let me take any of that for granted. Please help me to live like I really believe it.

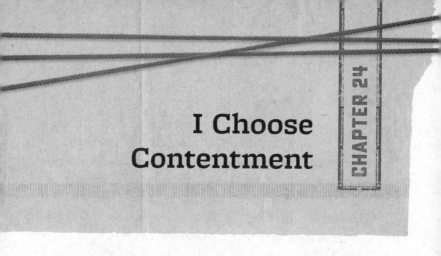

I Choose Contentment

I am not saying this because I am in need, for I have learned to be content whatever the circumstances. I know what it is to be in need, and I know what it is to have plenty. I have learned the secret of being content in any and every situation, whether well fed or hungry, whether living in plenty or in want. I can do all this through him who gives me strength. –Philippians 4:11–13

Do you ever have "win the lottery" fantasies? You imagine what you would do if you ever won the lottery. Yes! I don't even play the lottery, but I still have "win the lottery" fantasies.

Do you ever have "become a quadriplegic" fantasies? You imagine what you would do if you ever became quadriplegic? No?

Here's what's interesting: several studies have shown that people who become lottery winners and people who become quadriplegics have exactly the same level of happiness one year later. Why is that?

The Quest for More

My first job after college was at Abercrombie & Fitch. You know the guy standing out front with no shirt on? Yep, that *wasn't* me. I was the dude folding the clothes inside. I thought about taking off my shirt and standing at the entrance with the other guy but, well, I didn't want my abs to intimidate his. I'm just kind of humble about my abs like that. (And I didn't want people to throw up in their mouths on the way into the store.)

I got paid $23,000 a year at that job. I thought I was rich. I didn't know how I could possibly spend all that money. But pretty soon I realized it wasn't enough. I changed jobs and soon was making twice as much. Finally, I had enough! Until it wasn't. I later discovered that three times, and then five times, and even ten times as much, which I made in a business development job, wasn't enough. No matter how much I made, I wasn't happy and wanted more.

You might think I have a problem, and I might agree, but it turns out we *all* have this problem. A survey divided people by income groups, from people making millions to those on welfare. Each group was asked the same question, How much more money do you need to have enough? When the results came in, each group, *regardless of their current income*, gave a number that equated to about 23 percent more than they currently made. Even people making millions said they needed more, a significant amount more, to have enough.

We all think more will make us happy, but the people who have more confess that they're not happy. Ted Turner said, about becoming a billionaire, "Having great wealth is one of the most disappointing things I've ever experienced. It's overrated. I can tell you that."[1] Another wealthy man, Andrew Carnegie, said, "Millionaires who laugh are rare, very rare indeed."[2]

So, why do we all want more?

Contentment Instead of Coveting

One thing that makes us want more is comparison. We always compare ourselves to people who have more than we do. We eye the riches and possessions of others, then look at what we have and think, *It could be better*. That leads to, *I deserve better! I'm going to go buy something better! I'm going to live somewhere better!* Perhaps we do get better—we get more—and we're still not happy. Our new possessions may even lead to increased depression and desperation.

What if we memorized a new mantra and said it every time we think about what we have or don't have. It's easy to remember, just three words: "I choose contentment."

When you go out to your car and are tempted to think, *If I just had a bigger, nicer, newer, more expensive car, I'd be content*, you will, instead, say to yourself, *I choose contentment*.

When you walk up to your apartment or house and are tempted to think, *If I just had a bigger, nicer, newer, more expensive home, I'd be content*, you will, instead, say to yourself, *I choose contentment*.

If you know God and his unconditional love, if you have become the recipient of his amazing grace, if you have him with you every moment and know that you will go to be with him forever in his perfect heaven, you have *everything* you need to be content.

PONDER

Why is it so easy to focus on what we don't have and ignore what we do?

PRACTICE

Write down as many things as you can that you are thankful for. How long can you make that list?

PRAY

Father God, please forgive me for when I haven't been grateful. Forgive me for when I think too little of all the gifts you've given me and too much about what I don't have. I know the secret of contentment: I have everything I need in you. I can be content through Jesus, who gives me strength.

CHAPTER 25

Before You Face Your Giant

David said to Saul, "Let no one lose heart on account of this Philistine; your servant will go and fight him." Saul replied, "You are not able to go out against this Philistine and fight him; you are only a young man, and he has been a warrior from his youth." But David said to Saul, "Your servant has been keeping his father's sheep. When a lion or a bear came and carried off a sheep from the flock, I went after it, struck it and rescued the sheep from its mouth. When it turned on me, I seized it by its hair, struck it and killed it. Your servant has killed both the lion and the bear; this uncircumcised Philistine will be like one of them, because he has defied the armies of the living God. The Lord who rescued me from the paw of the lion and the paw of the bear will rescue me from the hand of this Philistine." Saul said to David, "Go, and the Lord be with you." –1 Samuel 17:32–37

You have a Goliath. We all do. By *Goliath*, I mean something standing in the way of you moving forward toward your destiny. You have a Goliath.

What's the giant you can't seem to get past?

You can defeat your Goliath. Perhaps you have come to a place where you feel like you'll never be able to overcome the giant. You can.

Actually, I take that back. You've already proven that you can't beat your Goliath. You can't. *But* you and God can. You and God, together, can defeat your Goliath.

David, when he was only a teenager, defeated the actual Goliath, a huge enemy warrior for the Philistine army. Check out the first thing we ever see David say: "David asked the men standing near him, 'What will be done for the man who kills this Philistine and removes this disgrace from Israel? Who is this uncircumcised Philistine that he should defy the armies of the living God?'" (1 Sam. 17:26).

Did you notice how confident David was that he would defeat Goliath? He knew he would win. He just wanted to know what the prize would be.

If you read the entire story, you will notice David referred to Goliath only two times but repeatedly talked about God. Isn't that interesting? From the time David lays eyes on Goliath, he can't stop talking about . . . God. David saw the giant; he just saw God more.

I wonder, with the giant you're facing: Are you staring more at it or at God?

I believe the key to David's victory was that his focus was not on his enemy but on God, and his faith was not in himself but in God. If you are going to overcome, you will have the same key to your victory.

How do we get that God-perspective David had? I notice two things from David's life.

Time Alone with God

Before facing Goliath, David was shepherding sheep alone in the fields. We see from David's writing in the Psalms that he used that time to think about and be with God. You can imagine David lying in the fields, looking up at the stars in the night sky, and being inspired to write, "The heavens declare the glory of God; the skies proclaim the work of his hands. Day after day they pour forth speech; night after night they reveal knowledge" (Ps. 19:1–2). David used his alone time to connect with God. No wonder, when faced with a giant bully, all he could think about was God.

If you want to beat your Goliath, you need to spend time alone with God in the fields.

I would suggest that means starting every day with God, to fix your focus on him for the rest of the day. The legendary boxer Joe Frazier once said, "Champions aren't made in the ring, they are merely recognized there. What you cheat on in the early light of morning will show up in the ring under the bright lights."[1] It's true. Victory isn't about the moment of battle, it's about all the moments you spent each morning preparing for the moment.

Start your day with God, and then try to use any extra time during the day to spend more time with him. Have a long drive to work? Awesome. Pray and listen to worship music. Have a job where you have big chunks of time with nothing to do? Awesome. Read your Bible.

To beat your giant, you first have to spend time alone with God in the fields.

Face Lions and Bears

David volunteered to fight Goliath. King Saul told him he was just a boy, not a soldier, and he was not up for the task of fighting Goliath. David responded,

> Your servant has been keeping his father's sheep. When a lion or a bear came and carried off a sheep from the flock, I went after it, struck it and rescued the sheep from its mouth. When it turned on me, I seized it by its hair, struck it and killed it. Your servant has killed both the lion and the bear; this uncircumcised Philistine will be like one of them, because he has defied the armies of the living God. The LORD who rescued me from the paw of the lion and the paw of the bear will rescue me from the hand of this Philistine. (1 Sam. 17:34–37)

David had been anointed to be the next king. That's huge! Then he . . . waited. He went back to the fields to be a shepherd. And, as a shepherd, he faced and defeated lions and bears.

No wonder, when faced with a giant bully, he assumed he would win.

If you want to beat your Goliath, you need to first face lions and bears. In fact, I think often God sends us lions and bears to prepare us to face giants in the future. The problem is that we sometimes walk away from the lion or bear because it's not the giant. Maybe you quit a job that becomes challenging because it's not your dream job, but what if "winning" in that job would have prepared you for your dream job?

Spend time with God in the fields and beat some lions and bears. Then you and God can *totally* defeat your Goliath.

PONDER

What "Goliath" are you facing or want to face and defeat?

PRACTICE

Identify a "lion" or "bear" that could develop you and give you the experience to prepare you to beat your Goliath. Commit to doing whatever it takes to beat that lion or bear.

PRAY

Lord, I want to have the same God-perspective David had. Please help me to spend lots of time looking at you, so eventually I see you everywhere I look. Give me the kind of confidence in you that David had. I know that, with you, I can do anything.

CHAPTER 26

Revolutionary Humility

All of you, clothe yourselves with humility toward one another, because, "God opposes the proud but shows favor to the humble." Humble yourselves, therefore, under God's mighty hand, that he may lift you up in due time.
–1 Peter 5:5–6

What if I told you that there is something which, if you get it, would: (1) Make you happier, (2) Lead other people to like and respect you more than they ever have, and (3) Get God on your side, advancing your cause, instead of having him actively working against you?

You would do *anything* to get whatever that was, right? I mean, those are some awesome benefits. Getting this "something" might become your highest priority.

Well, there is something you can get that will lead to those benefits. That something is *humility*.

What is humility? Some think to be humble means you view yourself as unimportant, untalented, and unworthy. But that's not it. A wise person once said, "Humility isn't thinking less of yourself, it's just thinking of yourself less." The apostle Paul wrote, "Do nothing out of selfish ambition or vain conceit. Rather, in humility value others above yourselves, not looking to your own interests but each of you to the interests of the others" (Phil. 2:3–4). Humility is moving "me" out of the center of the universe. It's deciding to put God first and others before myself. In our culture, living this way is pretty revolutionary, but it's the way Jesus lived, and we are called to follow his example (see vv. 5–11).

Are you humble? Here are a few questions to test yourself. What percentage of your thoughts yesterday were about you? How much do you care about how you look, what other people think of you, or your own performance? How much do you battle insecurity? How many great questions have you asked others and actually listened to their answers? How much do you show other people how important they are?

We need humility.

We don't live humbly for its benefits, but there are some amazing benefits to being humble.

Humility Makes You Happier

Jesus said, "Whoever finds their life will lose it, and whoever loses their life for my sake will find it" (Matt. 10:39). We are always trying to reach out and grab life and clutch it tightly in our greedy little fingers, but Jesus tells us when we let go of the things we think we need to be happy, we will finally find true happiness.

We've been taught that looking out for number one will make us happy, but the exact opposite is true. Selfishness *robs* us of happiness. It fuels comparison and steals contentment and compassion. Self*less*ness, living for others, makes us happier.

Humility Leads Others to Like and Respect You

You know that person who makes you feel special? They're always happy to see you. When they ask, "How are you?" you know they sincerely want to know, so you can't give the standard, "Good; how are you?" answer. You tell the truth because you know they care and will take time to listen.

What's different about that person? Humility. The secret to humility is remembering that it's not all about you. This person lives that way, and you get to experience it in your interactions with them.

How do you feel about that person? I bet you really like and respect them. Of course you do! How could you not?

If you live with humility, remembering that it's not about you, how do you think others would feel about you?

Humility Gets God on Your Side

Does God love you? Yes. Always. Unconditionally.

Is God on your side? Depends. Sometimes. Conditionally.

God is on your side, advancing your cause, lifting you up, *if* you are humble. But if you are proud—if your "why" is you instead of God and others, God will not be on your side.

"God opposes the proud
but shows favor to the humble."

Submit yourselves, then, to God. Resist the devil, and he will flee from you. Come near to God and he will come near to you. . . . Humble yourselves before the Lord, and he will lift you up. (James 4:6–10)

Having God opposed to you is a scary thought. I wonder if I've had times in my life where my motivation and goals were self-centered, so God opposed my progress. Perhaps you have an area of your life where you feel stuck, unable to get or sustain momentum. Could it be that God is opposing your success because the victory would be all about you?

The Error We Should Make

I know this can bring up a lot of questions. "When is it OK to do something just for me?" "What if my success is for me but will also benefit others?"

I don't know the answer to all those questions, but I do know God tells us to "clothe [ourselves] in humility" (1 Pet. 5:5).

Years ago, I had a job interview and didn't know if I should wear a suit or go more casual. I showed up in a suit, but everyone else was dressed business casual. I felt like I had made a mistake, but in my interview the CEO told me, "You erred to the right side."

Every time you are not sure of the answer or are not sure what to do, and you decide to choose humility, you are erring to the right side.

PONDER

Who is the most humble person you know? What makes that person special?

PRACTICE

Write down the goals you have for yourself—career, fitness, relationships, finances, all of it—and for each, ask yourself: *Is the reason I want that for myself or for God or others?* What does your list tell you about you?

PRAY

God, I want to follow Jesus's example and live a humble life. It's not easy. I have a selfishness that is hard to overcome. Please help me. Help me to give up my life—in serving you and others—so I can find the life you have for me.

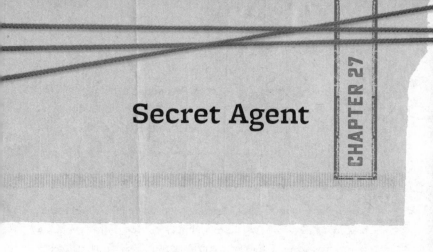

Secret Agent

Slaves, obey your earthly masters in everything; and do it, not only when their eye is on you and to curry their favor, but with sincerity of heart and reverence for the Lord. Whatever you do, work at it with all your heart, as working for the Lord, not for human masters, since you know that you will receive an inheritance from the Lord as a reward. It is the Lord Christ you are serving. –Colossians 3:22–24

Did you see *The Informant!*? It is a 2009 movie based on a true story, starring Matt Damon as Mark Whitacre. Whitacre worked for ADM, a food processing company. He went to the FBI with information about illegal price-fixing his company was involved in. The FBI asked Whitacre to serve as an undercover agent, secretly gathering evidence to build a criminal case against the ADM executives. He enthusiastically jumped into the role, telling a friend he had become "Mark Whitacre, secret agent 00-14." When asked, "Why 00-14?" he responded, "Because I'm twice as smart as 00-7."

Imagine yourself in Mark's shoes. Becoming a double agent probably infused purpose into every moment of his workday, don't you think? His job didn't change, but he was now on a mission from a higher authority.

The Undercover Agent

Now imagine yourself in *your* shoes. You have a job, or will someday. I don't know how you feel about your job, but if you are a follower of Jesus, I know the truth about it. The truth is: you are working for a higher authority and have a higher purpose.

You Are Working for a Higher Authority

You may work for the school district, a factory, or in retail, but regardless of who sets your schedule or signs your paychecks, the reality is that you work for God. He is your true boss. "Whatever you do, work at it with all your heart, as working for the Lord, not for human masters. . . . It is the Lord Christ you are serving" (Col. 3:23–24). That's a game changer! You may not like your boss, and that can be demotivating, but you love Jesus, and knowing he is your boss is motivating!

Your Work Has a Higher Purpose

I hope you find a job where you love what you do, but that is not necessary for you to have great passion for your work. Today, we are obsessed with using tests like the Enneagram, StrengthsFinder, and Myers-Briggs to identify how we're wired so we can find a job that is the right "fit" for us. The apostle Paul made tents for a living. Was it because he was "wired" to make tents? I doubt it. He made tents to support his mission. The primary reason we go to work is to support our mission, and also because our workplace is our mission field.

What's our mission? God has "committed to us the message of reconciliation. We are therefore Christ's ambassadors, as though God were making his appeal through us. We implore you on Christ's behalf: Be reconciled to God" (2 Cor. 5:19–20). Our mission is to represent God and to help people at our jobs put their faith in Jesus so they can be reconciled to God.

How do we do that? We need to blend in.

Blend In

At work, we should blend in. Meaning we don't separate ourselves from sinful people. If we're not developing relationships and hanging out with people who are far from God, we'll never be able to help them get close to God.

So, we blend in, but we also stand out.

Stand Out

We do not blend in when it comes to joining in sinful conversations or activities. If people at work are gossiping, we graciously choose *not* to blend in. If people are going to a strip club after work, we graciously choose *not* to blend in.

We need people to see the difference God has made in our lives, so they will want God to make that difference in their lives too.

Paul wrote that we are to "make the teaching about God our Savior attractive" (Titus 2:10). How do we make God attractive? We can

> Do everything without grumbling or arguing, so that you may become blameless and pure, "children of God without fault in a warped and crooked generation." Then you will shine among them like stars in the sky as you hold firmly to the word of life. (Phil. 2:14–16)

We *do* separate ourselves from sinful conversations and activities, but we do *not* separate ourselves from sinful people.

How do we accomplish our mission? We blend in, we stand out, and we talk to God and about God.

Talk to God and about God

God gave us a mission and a mission field. We know we can't accomplish our mission without God's help, and we know that to accomplish our mission, people need to hear about Jesus. Therefore, we have to talk to God about the people we work with and talk to the people we work with about God.

> Devote yourselves to prayer, being watchful and thankful. And pray for us, too, that God may open a door for our message, so that we may proclaim the mystery of Christ, for which I am in chains. Pray that I may proclaim it clearly, as I should. Be wise in the way you act toward outsiders; make the most of every opportunity. Let your conversation be always full of grace, seasoned with salt, so that you may know how to answer everyone. (Col. 4:2–6)

When you talk to people at work, you don't have to make it weird—no judgment, no religious language. Look for chances to share who God is and what he's been doing in your life. You'll be surprised at how receptive most people are, if you've first made God "attractive" through how you've lived your life.

You can do this. Why? Because God will be with you . . . and you're twice as smart as 00-7.

PONDER

In what (good or bad) ways do you blend in at work? In what ways do you stand out?

PRACTICE

Pick someone at work (or in your class at school) to pray for, right now, and to invite to go out to lunch this week (to deepen your relationship and, if you have a chance, to start a spiritual conversation).

PRAY

God, help me to remember my mission when I go to work. I want the people I work with to know you and go to heaven with me. Please use me as your ambassador and make your appeal through me.

CHAPTER 28

A Day of Rest

Humble yourselves before the Lord, and he will lift you up. –James 4:10

Today there is no reading, as it's a day of rest. However, the day is not without God. We rest with God, seeking to fill ourselves with him.

We've already learned how God values humility. What would it look like for you to truly humble yourself before the Lord today, and, if you did, how do you think he might lift you up?

CHAPTER 29

Worried for No Reason

Therefore I tell you, do not worry about your life, what you will eat or drink; or about your body, what you will wear. Is not life more than food, and the body more than clothes? Look at the birds of the air; they do not sow or reap or store away in barns, and yet your heavenly Father feeds them. Are you not much more valuable than they? Can any one of you by worrying add a single hour to your life? –Matthew 6:25–27

I would like to propose a motto for my generation. Here it is:

"Worried for No Reason"

I'm not suggesting it's a good thing. I just think it's real.

Statistically, we're a worrisome bunch. According to the World Health Organization, America is the most anxious country in the world, with one-third of us suffering from an anxiety disorder at some point in our lives.[1] Within this anxious country, young adults are the most anxious of all; more than half of Millennials report that they've lost sleep and lain awake at night in the past month due to stress.[2]

It might not seem like a serious problem, but it is a big deal. Big enough that we spend a couple billion dollars a year on medications to try to manage it.[3] But you don't have to reach the point of a medical diagnosis for it to impact your health. A British study of over sixty-eight thousand people found that even low levels of worry can literally kill you. People with mild symptoms of anxiety, such as occasionally lying awake at night worrying, were 20 percent more likely to die within the ten-year period covered by the study.[4] Jesus asked, in Matthew 6:27, "Can any one of you by worrying add a single hour to your life?" The answer, clearly, is no.

Now you're probably worrying about the fact that you worry. Let's stop the madness. What should we do about this problem? We wage war on worry. Here's how.

Remember God Is in Control

My daughter Presley loved to go to the grocery store when she was younger. We would get the grocery cart that had a little car attached to the front. The car had a steering wheel that didn't actually steer anything. Presley would sit in the car and loved to think she was driving. I would steer in whatever direction she did to add to the illusion she was in control. But eventually, Presley would steer left and I would steer right. She wouldn't like it, but I had to frustrate her because I had an agenda. There were things we needed to do, and her steering would not get us there. Whenever I finally steered in the opposite direction, the realization would hit Presley that she was *not* in control.

We're a lot like my daughter in that pretend driver's seat. We live the fantasy that we're masters of our fate, steering to our destiny, but the reality is that God is in control. That's a good thing. It means we really have nothing to worry about. Jesus said that our heavenly Father knows what we need (Matt. 6:8) and that, like any good father, he will give us the good things we need if we just ask (7:7–11). Check what Jesus said about worry in Matthew 6:31–32.

> So do not worry, saying, "What shall we eat?" or "What shall we drink?" or "What shall we wear?" For the pagans run after all these things, and your heavenly Father knows that you need them.

A "pagan" is someone who doesn't know God. Jesus was saying that it makes sense to worry *if* we don't know God. But if we have a heavenly Father, there is no need to worry.

God's job is to take care of us. Jesus said, in Matthew 6:33, that our job is to "seek first his kingdom and his righteousness."

Remember That God Is Good

God is in control, which is good if God is good. You wouldn't want to rely on God if he wasn't trustworthy. That's why the word *righteousness* in that last verse is so important. To be righteous is to be "morally right or justifiable." What God does is right. Everything he does is justifiable, because he has a plan and is working for the greater good.

Time and time again in my life, and in the lives of others, I've seen God take something bad and make it good. I bet you have too. Even still, sometimes when you're in the middle of something bad, it can be difficult to see the good God can bring out of it. That's when you have to trust.

Remember, when Jesus was tortured and killed as a criminal, it looked like the worst, most unfair event in history. But God was in control even then, and he used it to bring about the greatest good in history.

Take One Day at a Time

In the next verse in Matthew 6, Jesus said, "Therefore do not worry about tomorrow, for tomorrow will worry about itself. Each day has enough trouble of its own" (v. 34).

I have decided to give my worries a twelve-hour boundary. If what I'm thinking of is not coming up in the next twelve hours, I don't worry about it. I might prepare for it, if needed, but I refuse to let myself worry about it.

Most of the things we worry about don't end up happening, so not allowing ourselves to worry about the future is a wise choice. If it does end up happening, I'll deal with it when the time comes, but by not worrying in advance I'll be happier and more productive.

What if we make a decision today to change our motto from "Worried for No Reason" to "Trusting God with Good Reason"?

PONDER

What do you find yourself worrying about most? Why do you think you worry about it?

PRACTICE

Memorize Matthew 6:34 and recite it whenever you are tempted to worry: "Therefore do not worry about tomorrow, for tomorrow will worry about itself. Each day has enough trouble of its own."

PRAY

God, I know you are good and that I can trust you. I want to *really* trust you. If I do, I know I won't feel the need to worry. Please help me.

CHAPTER 30

The Antidote for Anxiety

Humble yourselves, therefore, under God's mighty hand, that he may lift you up in due time. Cast all your anxiety on him because he cares for you. Be alert and of sober mind. Your enemy the devil prowls around like a roaring lion looking for someone to devour. Resist him, standing firm in the faith, because you know that the family of believers throughout the world is undergoing the same kind of sufferings. And the God of all grace, who called you to his eternal glory in Christ, after you have suffered a little while, will himself restore you and make you strong, firm and steadfast. –1 Peter 5:6–10

Every year, my ministry put on an event for about one thousand young adults. When the event was over, we would have to pick up and stack the metal folding chairs. One thousand metal folding chairs is a *lot* of metal folding chairs. A bunch of us would start grabbing chairs and carrying them to the stacks. You would see less-muscular people carrying two or maybe four chairs at a time.

Some people would carry six chairs, hoping to get home sooner. Then there would be a few big dudes trying to show off for the girls by carrying ten chairs at a time. Invariably, in the middle of our work, a loud crash would startle everyone. We didn't have to look up because we all knew what had happened. Someone had tried to carry more chairs than they could handle and dropped all of them.

I think of anxiety like that. Anxiety is a sign that we have been trying to carry too much. Anxiety tells us that something is off in our lives.

When My Burden Became Too Much

A few years ago, my life got away from me. The ministry I was leading exploded to tens of thousands of people showing up on Tuesday nights, listening to messages online, and emailing me from all over the country. Requests to speak at other churches and conferences increased exponentially. At the same time, my job responsibilities were changing. Then I lost a valued coworker. My kids were young, and their sports seasons were in full swing. Then a loved one became ill, and I had to give them a lot of attention and care.

Something broke inside of me. It was like I had been carrying ten chairs but now had twenty. I couldn't support the burden. I wasn't able to sleep. I was tired all the time. I couldn't focus; my mind was always racing. One night I lay in bed with my head tingling and my heart beating erratically.

That was when I began to understand the difference between worry and anxiety. I'm no doctor, but I would say that if worry is like a bicycle horn, then anxiety is like a horn on an eighteen-wheeler. If worry is like a cold, then anxiety is like the flu.

I saw a therapist and was given a prescription for an antianxiety medication. Before taking it, I tried two things. If you struggle with anxiety, I would encourage you to see a doctor or Christian counselor, and a prescription may be helpful to get you through your difficult time. But I would also ask you to consider taking the two steps I did. Neither will provide a quick fix, because there is no quick fix, but they got me through my painful time, and I believe they'll help you.

Faithful Obedience One Step at a Time

When you're worried, anxious, or depressed, your feelings will betray you. You will be tempted to stop doing the things you need to be doing. Spiritual habits you've practiced in the past—reading the Bible, showing up at church, participating in a small group, praying—will feel like drudgery. You need to keep doing what you know you should regardless of how you feel about doing it.

You will also be tempted to stop believing things you need to believe. You will wonder if God is real or if he's really for you. You need to keep focusing on what you *know* is true even if it doesn't *feel* true.

> Finally, brothers and sisters, whatever is true, whatever is noble, whatever is right, whatever is pure, whatever is lovely, whatever is admirable—if anything is excellent or praiseworthy—think about such things. Whatever you have learned or received or heard from me, or seen in me—put it into practice. And the God of peace will be with you. (Phil. 4:8–9)

Meditation

In 1989, Dick and Carolyn received the news every parent dreads. Their twenty-seven-year-old son had died in a car accident. They plunged into a really dark place.

Their church encouraged them to go to counseling and get in a support group. They did, and it helped, but not enough. All the encouraging words started to ring hollow. Dick and Carolyn didn't know what to do. Then they read a book called *Healing into Life and Death* by Stephen Levine. The book led them to a retreat where they could learn about and try something called Centering Prayer. They had never heard of it but were open to anything that might help them with their pain.

The aim of Centering Prayer is not to talk to God but to "be still and know God." The goal is to eliminate distractions, to achieve an inner silence, and to become very aware of and experience God's presence. The method of Centering Prayer is to choose a single word, like *love*, *Jesus*, *abide*, or *God*, and to meet every distracting thought with that word. When your mind becomes distracted, you use the word to bring your focus back to God. When your focus is on God, you just sit quietly with him, feeling his presence and love.

Dick and Carolyn learned this ancient method of prayer and started practicing it consistently, and everything changed. Dick said, "After three years of daily Centering Prayer, the pain was gone. I still miss my son, but the pain, loss, and grief that had paralyzed me for three years miraculously lifted. And the same thing happened to Carolyn."[1]

That's my story too. In the midst of my anxiety I was encouraged to try meditating. For a Christian, meditating is deep, still, contemplative prayer. God tells us, in Psalm 46:10, "Be still, and know that I am God." Meditating is eliminating distractions and focusing on knowing God and knowing God is with us. When we do that, we will begin to experience his peace.

Do not be anxious about anything, but in every situation, by prayer and petition, with thanksgiving, present your requests to God. And the peace of God, which transcends all understanding, will guard your hearts and your minds in Christ Jesus. (Phil. 4:6–7)

PONDER

What has been your response when you've struggled with anxiety? Did it help?

PRACTICE

Turn everything off (yes, even your phone) for a few minutes and try Centering Prayer.

PRAY

Father God, you tell me to not be anxious about anything, so I believe that's possible. I want to turn all of my anxious thoughts over to you and experience your peace that passes understanding.

CHAPTER 31

The Warning Signal of Anger

> My dear brothers and sisters, take note of this: Everyone should be quick to listen, slow to speak and slow to become angry, because human anger does not produce the righteousness that God desires. –James 1:19–20

Much of my life has been marked by outbursts of anger. Anger has kept me from living at peace with myself and with others.

Something would happen. My temperature would rise. I would explode. My words would spill out, totally out of control. The relationship would end. In fact, to this day I am still trying to reconcile with some former friends.

My anger problem only began to change when I started following Christ. Jesus had some pretty strong things to say about anger.

> You have heard that it was said to the people long ago, "You shall not murder, and anyone who murders will be subject to judgment." But I tell you that anyone who is angry with a brother or sister will be subject to judgment. Again, anyone who says

to a brother or sister, "Raca," is answerable to the court. And anyone who says, "You fool!" will be in danger of the fire of hell. (Matt. 5:21–22)

Jesus equates anger with murder. Murder is punishable by death. Jesus is saying my outbursts of anger are punishable by death. I am grateful that Jesus took my punishment for me, but that does not mean I can take the sin of anger lightly.

Responding to Anger

Anger is an emotion. It can be difficult to control emotions. However, we can control what we do in response to the feeling of anger. God said, "in your anger do not sin" (Eph. 4:26). There is a sinful way to deal with our anger and a *non*-sinful way.

I find it helpful to think of anger as a warning signal, like the "check engine" light in the car. When that bad boy comes on, we have three options.

One, we can ignore it. If we do, that means we are ignoring the problem, which will only get worse. Eventually, we will be stranded on the side of the road.

Two, we can overreact to it. The check engine light came on? Well, so much for that car. Pull over, push it into a ditch, and walk home.

Three, we can find the problem and get it fixed.

Clearly, the third option is the only one that makes sense. It's the only logical thing to do. It is also the option that will take the most time and work.

The same is true when we feel angry. The best option is to work through it to find the root of the problem. Don't ignore it and don't overreact and explode. Figure out what's wrong and resolve the issue.

How? Here are some ideas for dealing with anger.

Own Your Part

When we feel anger toward someone else, we are often blind to our part of the problem. You need to own your part. It may be that 99 percent of the issue is not your fault. Still, own your part. Own 100 percent of that 1 percent.

Overlook What You Can

If what the other person did really is not a big deal, choose to forget about it. "It is to one's glory to overlook an offense" (Prov. 19:11).

You may be wondering, *But how do I know if it is small enough to overlook?* It is small enough to overlook if you can overlook it. If you can't forget about it, you need to resolve it.

Whatever You Feed Grows

Anger is like the little lion cub someone wants to keep as a pet. It doesn't seem like a problem—until you feed it and it grows, and then you have an issue on your hands.

So, you have an initial feeling of anger. That may not be a significant problem, but it will become one if you feed it. Every time you have another bitter thought, each time you imagine how you would yell at them, whenever you hope they are "paying for their sins," you are feeding your anger. It will grow, and eventually it will devour you.

We need to pay close attention to what we pay attention to. The Bible tells us to "take captive every thought to make it obedient to Christ" (2 Cor. 10:5). We choose what we think about. We need to grab all our angry thoughts and bring them to Jesus.

If You Seek to Win, You Lose

"Winning" an argument used to make me feel good. But later I would realize that I'd lost a friend or lost my ability to share God's love with someone I cared about. Don't try to win; seek to resolve the conflict and restore peace in your relationship.

Resolving Conflict Is Costly, but Not Resolving It Is More Costly

Do you know who enjoys having the hard conversations that resolve conflict? No one. We all go in nervous—there's a chance the other person will not take it well, there's a chance you'll get burned. The only thing worse than having to resolve conflict is *not* resolving conflict.

Only Talk to People Who Are Part of the Problem or Solution

When you are angry, it is easy to gossip about the other person or complain about them. You might be tempted to vent on social media. Don't do it. Jesus says we are to go directly to the person. We only bring another person into it if we need a mediator to help resolve the situation (see Matt. 18:15–16).

Conflict Is an Opportunity to Show Who You Belong To

When you are someone's child, you display their characteristics. For example, I'm six-foot-seven, so my kids are tall for their ages. If we truly want to be God's people, we must strive to take on his characteristics. Here's an important one. Jesus said, "Blessed are the peacemakers, for they will be called children of God" (Matt. 5:9).

Peacemakers are called God's children because they display one of God's chief characteristics. God had every right to be angry, but he pursued peace with us. Bringing peace cost him the life of his Son. He considered peace worth paying that price.

When you feel angry, it is one of the greatest opportunities you have to display your faith. You, like your heavenly Father, can pursue peace even if it costs you.

PONDER

When was the last time you felt angry? How did you deal with it? Did it show your faith?

PRACTICE

Is there someone with whom you need to resolve conflict? Someone you need to apologize to?

PRAY

Thank you, Father, for offering me peace when my sin had made you angry. Please don't let me receive that from you and not offer it to others. Help me to never sin in my anger and to always be a peacemaker.

CHAPTER 32

If It's Not Good, God's Not Done

And we know that in all things God works for the good of those who love him, who have been called according to his purpose. –Romans 8:28

A few years ago, we had a gifted painter complete a work of art on stage during one of our services. When he finished, everyone looked at the painting with great anticipation, but they were greatly disappointed. It was a nonsensical, ugly mess of paint.

Do you ever feel like that with God? You look with great expectation at your life, at the outcomes of things you prayed for, but it seems that God has made a mess of your situation. You try to make sense of it but all you see is nonsense.

Romans 8:28 is, arguably, the most hopeful and encouraging verse in the Bible when it comes to living in a fallen world. It's so positive it can come across as a trite religious platitude. The hope this verse offers, however, is a deep well of truth that is anything but cliché. Let's dig in deep and discover why this verse can be such a powerful help.

And We Know

Notice it says, "we know." We don't assume or hope this is true; we *know* it. It's a reality God proclaimed that has been verified thousands of times in the Bible, in people's lives ever since, and in my life personally.

That in All Things God Works

God is at work in all things. That is an amazing truth. It means that God has not left you to flail helplessly through life. He spoke you into existence, formed you in your mother's womb, and has numbered the days of your life. God has a plan, and he is at work in all your circumstances and situations.

For the Good

God is at work, and he is not laboring in vain. He is intentionally working toward an end goal. God is in the process of accomplishing something that *will* be good for you.

We may need to redefine what is good. We'll try to do that in a bit.

Of Those Who Love Him, Who Have Been Called According to His Purpose

This promise is not available to everyone. It is reserved for those who love God and have been awakened to the reality that God has a purpose and they are a part of it.

Does that describe you? Do you acknowledge that God's plans are more important than yours, and do you want to be a part of them? If so, God is working in everything in your life to bring out something good.

This isn't, "Everything happens for a reason." There's not much truth, and no hope, in that statement. A "reason" isn't necessarily good. What God is doing is good. So let's try to understand what *good* is.

Redefining Good

The good God is about is described in the verses that follow Romans 8:28.

> For those God foreknew he also predestined to be conformed to the image of his Son, that he might be the firstborn among many brothers and sisters. And those he predestined, he also called; those he called, he also justified; those he justified, he also glorified. (vv. 29–30)

The good is glory. God's children will be glorified, like Jesus, for all eternity. God is preparing eternal blessings for you.

How good is that?! There is a reward at the end of your faithful perseverance. It's like working out. People go to the gym, where they sweat and suffer, because they have a desired end goal. Without the reward, they would quit. God is telling us there is eternal benefit for the suffering we go through in this life.

Honestly, at the risk of sounding calloused, your suffering won't matter one hundred years from now, except for how you have benefited from it. You'll actually be *glad* you endured it because of the good it produced for you and in you.

Remember the artist who painted a disappointing, ugly mess during our church service?

After everyone had a chance to look at it, I flipped it over, revealing that it was actually an amazing painting of the face of Jesus. The artist had painted it upside down. People gasped in awe and applauded. What looked ugly was actually beautiful. What appeared bad was actually good.

That's the promise God gives us in Romans 8:28. Whatever you go through, God will use it to make you look more like Jesus. *That* is the ultimate good.

Right now, you may be looking at an ugly mess, and you can't see how God is going to make something good of it. "How can this breakup be good?" "How can being unemployed and having huge school loans be good?" "How can cancer be good?" I don't know. I don't know how it is making you more like Jesus, but I know it is.

When I struggle to see how God can bring good out of a bad situation, I think about the day Jesus was tortured, nailed to a cross, and died a humiliating death. It seemed like the worst day ever, but we now call it "Good Friday." Why? Because we have received more good from that day than any other in all of history. God flipped the painting.

Whatever you may be going through, hold on to Romans 8:28. It may be an ugly mess now, but God is going to flip the painting.

PONDER

When have you seen God bring good out of a bad situation?

PRACTICE

Put Romans 8:28 on a 3x5 card or piece of notepaper. Carry it with you, starting today, and read it whenever you have a chance (at a red light, in line at the grocery store, and so on) until you have it memorized.

PRAY

Lord, when things seem bad they just seem bad, but I know the truth: you will bring good out of the bad. Help me to love you and to always want to accomplish your purpose. Help me to trust that you are in control and have a good plan for me.

CHAPTER 33

That's Not a Donut, It's Grace

For the grace of God has appeared that offers salvation to all people. It teaches us to say "No" to ungodliness and worldly passions, and to live self-controlled, upright and godly lives in this present age, while we wait for the blessed hope—the appearing of the glory of our great God and Savior, Jesus Christ, who gave himself for us to redeem us from all wickedness and to purify for himself a people that are his very own, eager to do what is good
–Titus 2:11–14

My daughter Presley is almost always a very good girl. I am proud to call her mine. I feel the need to point that out, because I am about to tell you a story of when she was not a very good girl.

One day, when Presley was about five years old, she hit her sister, Finley. They typically get along great, and violence is not normal in our home. This was totally out of character.

Presley knew she had no chance of getting away with it because I was there. I watched it happen. She looked at me with fear. I knew she was thinking, *Oh no, what is Daddy gonna do?*

I had no idea what I was going to do. Children don't come with an instruction manual, and I had never dealt with my kids hitting each other. I started praying, asking God to tell me what to say.

I picked Presley up and carried her out to my truck. Presley started crying and saying, "I'm sorry, Daddy. I'm sorry. I'm sorry."

I started driving. My guess is, Presley was thinking I was going to give her away or something. We drove to our family's donut shop. (We don't own the donut shop. We just eat a *lot* of donuts there. Come to think of it, it would probably be better for us financially if we *did* own the donut shop.)

We walked inside, and I ordered Presley her favorite chocolate éclair. Presley had big, confused eyes. She wiped tears away, looking at the éclair, and probably wondered if maybe it was her last meal.

We sat down and I asked her, "What did you do?"

She looked afraid again. "I hit my sister."

"What do you deserve?" I asked.

"A spanking."

"Yes, you deserve the spanking of a lifetime. I can't believe you hit your sister like that. That's not who you are."

Then I pointed to the éclair. "What's this?"

"That's a donut," she said.

"No, Presley, that's grace."

Grace

I told my daughter to eat the donut and to enjoy it. She took her first bite, very suspiciously.

I explained, "Grace means to get the opposite of the consequence you deserve. That's what God has done for your daddy. Daddy deserved the spanking of a lifetime. But God has shown me grace. When Jesus went to the cross, he took my spanking. He absorbed my punishment and gave me abundant life and an eternal future in heaven in place of it. So, Presley, enjoy your donut. That's grace."

To receive grace means to get the opposite of what is deserved, and grace means *everything*. It is the key to us having peace in this life and peace after this life.

Grace is getting the opposite of what we deserve from God, but we try to deserve it.

We think if we feel badly enough about what we've done and tell God "I'm sorry" enough, he might begrudgingly tolerate us. We think if we stop doing so much bad stuff, and do enough good stuff, we might end up on the right side of his almighty balance sheet.

No. That's not how it works. God offers to save us through grace. We can be restored into a relationship with him and be with him for all eternity because of grace. "For it is by grace you have been saved, through faith—and this is not from yourselves, it is the gift of God—not by works, so that no one can boast" (Eph. 2:8–9).

Grace is not just what gets us "saved." It is also the key to our transformation.

We think if we get disciplined and grit our teeth and try hard enough, maybe we can stop sinning. We think if we just understand God's wrath and fear the eternal consequence of hell, maybe we can say no to temptation.

No. That's not how it works. God offers to transform us through grace. "Or do you show contempt for the riches of his kindness, forbearance and patience, not realizing that God's kindness is intended to lead you to repentance?" (Rom. 2:4). We will want to stop sinning when we realize how much he loves us, that he gives us an éclair when we deserve punishment. But if we are ever going to change, it will only be because of grace.

If you want to stop striving, to be freed of the burden of your past sin and future transformation, you need to get your head around grace. It's hard to do because this type of exchange—abundant life and eternity in perfect heaven given for our sins—does not make sense. It doesn't feel natural. That's right. It isn't. It's supernatural, and we should feel super grateful.

PONDER

Is your motivation for not sinning and for doing good generally fear of God or love for God?

PRACTICE

Memorize Ephesians 2:8–9. Use it to motivate yourself and to share with others who need to be saved by God's grace.

PRAY

God, thank you for your grace. Please help me to understand it and live in it. I want to remember it, focus on it, and be motivated by it every moment of my life.

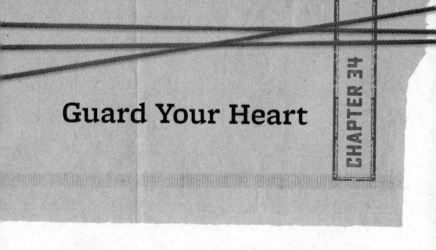

CHAPTER 34

Guard Your Heart

Make a tree good and its fruit will be good, or make a tree bad and its fruit will be bad, for a tree is recognized by its fruit. You brood of vipers, how can you who are evil say anything good? For the mouth speaks what the heart is full of. A good man brings good things out of the good stored up in him, and an evil man brings evil things out of the evil stored up in him. –Matthew 12:33–35

Proverbs is a book of wisdom for life. You should read it. You will see that one of its major themes is your heart. The word *heart* appears more than seventy-five times. Proverbs is written in Hebrew, and the word *heart* literally means the "kernel of the nut." Interesting, but not very romantic. Can you picture a guy telling his girl, "I love you with all the kernel of my nut"? I think we should probably stick with *heart*.

One's heart refers to the core of who they are. That's why Proverbs speaks of it so often. "As water reflects the face, so one's life reflects the heart" (Prov. 27:19). Our hearts define us.

They determine who we are, what we do, what we say, and how we act.

Guard Your Heart

All of this is why we're told, in Proverbs 4:23, "Above all else, guard your heart, for everything you do flows from it."

Everything flows from our hearts. We focus on our behavior, but our attention should be on our hearts. You might think you have a worrying problem; no, you've got a heart problem. You might think you have a pornography problem; no, you've got a heart problem. You might think you have a gambling or eating or gossip problem; no, you've got a heart problem.

People try to change what they do, but it just amounts to surface-level behavior modification. The issue is our hearts, and real change needs to happen from the inside out.

This is why we need to guard our hearts. In a book filled with hundreds of the wisest pieces of advice ever written, this is the only one preceded by the phrase "above all else."

But *how* do we guard our hearts?

Garbage In, Garbage Out

With your physical heart, blood flows in and blood flows out.

With your "spiritual" heart, if you fill it with good things, good things will flow out of it. If garbage flows in, garbage flows out. In fact, if you feed it with garbage, it will develop an appetite for garbage. There's an old saying: "The heart wants what it wants." No, the heart wants what it's fed.

For example, if you've struggled with pornography you know that giving in and looking at porn just one time only makes you desire it even more. Each time you look, it becomes easier to look again. That's why to overcome a pornography addiction you have to remove all access. You have to guard your heart.

Another example: after speaking at The Porch I will often have single women ask for help with their problem of "Only dating losers." In response, I ask what seems like a random question: "What are your favorite TV shows and songs?" The answers are usually those that portray, or even glorify, dating those types of guys. You have to guard your heart.

Guarding our hearts is all about being careful.

Be Careful What You Talk About

We all have conversations without thinking much about our words. But Proverbs 4:24 instructs us, "Keep your mouth free of perversity; keep corrupt talk far from your lips." What you talk about can feed your heart. If you share lustful thoughts with others, or gossip, or speak angry words, you need to understand that those words both flow out of your heart *and* feed your heart with garbage.

Be Careful What You Listen To

A theme throughout Proverbs is *listen*. Over and over, we are instructed to "Listen." "Listen." Why? Because what you hear flows into your heart and out into your life. "My son, pay attention to what I say; turn your ear to my words. Do not let them out of your sight, keep them within your heart; for they are life to those who find them and health to one's whole body" (vv. 20–22).

We think we don't need to be concerned with the music we listen to or with hearing gossip or off-color joking at work. Our justification might be, "I'm not the one doing it. I'm just listening." But no; something is happening to us, because our ears are the gateway to our hearts.

Be Careful What You Look At

What or who are you watching? Too often we are entertained by the very things Christ died for. The things you see and watch are flowing into your heart and influencing who you are and what you do far more than you realize. You need to be careful what you look at. "Let your eyes look straight ahead; fix your gaze directly before you" (v. 25).

Be Careful Where You Go

Guarding your heart may require changing where you hang out and who you hang out with. Being in the wrong places can expose you to the wrong things. This exposure gives those wrong things access into your heart. That's why you need to "Give careful thought to the paths for your feet and be steadfast in all your ways" (v. 26).

A Healthy Diet

Everything you do flows from your heart, and what flows *from* your heart is what previously flowed *into* it. It's garbage in, garbage out.

It's also good in, good out. So, in place of "garbage," feed your heart a healthy diet of the things of God. Read and memorize Scripture. Pray. Listen to worship music. Build deep relationships with other Christ-followers through community. You'll find your heart changing, and your life will quickly follow.

PONDER

If you had to estimate, what percentage of the things you are exposed to (internet, music, conversations, TV shows, and movies) would you say qualifies as "garbage," and what percentage qualifies as "good" or "godly"? What impact do you see that having in your life?

PRACTICE

Pick one "garbage" input you will cut (or greatly decrease) from your life. Pick one "godly" input you will start having (or greatly increase) in your life.

PRAY

God, I'm afraid I might ignore my heart too much. I think a lot about what I say and do, not realizing these flow from my heart. I'm also not careful enough about what flows into my heart. Please help me to guard my heart, Lord.

CHAPTER 35

A Day of Rest

Do not be anxious about anything, but in every situation, by prayer and petition, with thanksgiving, present your requests to God. And the peace of God, which transcends all understanding, will guard your hearts and your minds in Christ Jesus. –Philippians 4:6–7

This week we learned that we don't need to worry because we have a good Father, and we can cast all our cares on him because he cares about us.

Today is a day of rest—no reading—but why don't you spend some time talking to God about whatever is on your mind, knowing that he is listening and that he loves you?

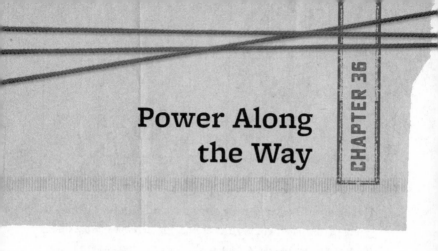

CHAPTER 36

Power Along the Way

I pray that the eyes of your heart may be enlightened in order that you may know the hope to which he has called you, the riches of his glorious inheritance in his holy people, and his incomparably great power for us who believe. That power is the same as the mighty strength he exerted when he raised Christ from the dead and seated him at his right hand in the heavenly realms. –Ephesians 1:18–20

God is powerful.
You know that.
You may, at times, feel powerless.
You know that too.

But do you realize God is willing to share his power with you? God wants you to experience transformation, live a new life, and make a difference in the world, and he will provide the power you need.

Along the Way

God's power is available, but many people never experience it because they don't know how to access it. How do we? Along the way.

In the book of Exodus, we find Moses leading thousands of Israelites out of Egypt. The Egyptian army is pursuing them. They end up at the Red Sea. They can't cross it. They realize they're going to die. The people start crying out to Moses. Moses tells them to keep walking, to walk to the water's edge. It didn't make sense, but the people did it. As they walked to the water's edge, God parted the Red Sea, and the Israelites walked right through it. God gave them his power *along the way*. He parted the Red Sea once they showed the faith to begin taking the action he'd asked them to take. He parted the water once they got their feet wet.

In the book of Joshua, the Israelites have been wandering through the wilderness for a whole generation. They've been waiting to get into the land God had promised them. Finally, just about there, they encountered a problem. The Jordan River. It was in front of them, and they couldn't cross it. Worse, the river was at flood stage. God told the people to keep moving. He told them to walk into that rushing river. I imagine everyone was afraid and parents put floaties on their kids, but they did it. As they walked into the water, trusting God would supernaturally take care of them, God parted the river and they walked through on dry land. God gave them power *along the way*. As they moved forward in faith, God did what they needed him to do.

In the book of Luke, we meet ten outcasts who were dying slowly of a disease called leprosy. They saw Jesus coming and cried out to him, "Jesus, Master, have pity on us!" Jesus responded, "Go, show yourselves to the priests" (Luke 17:13–14). That was kind of . . . odd. At the time the priests served as the health department and would verify if a person had been healed. These lepers would go to the priests if they were healed, but they *weren't* healed yet. The lepers were probably wondering, *We haven't been healed, so why would we go show ourselves to the priests?* But they mustered up the faith to obey Jesus even though it didn't make sense. We're told, "And as they were going, they were cleansed" (v. 14 NASB).

They experienced God's power "as they were going." It happened along the way.

God provides his power once we demonstrate faith in him by doing what he has asked us to do. The Bible says in Romans 15:13, "May the God of hope fill you with all joy and peace as you trust in him, so that you may overflow with hope by the power of the Holy Spirit." God comes through for us *as* we trust in him. He gives his power along the way.

Take the Step

I wonder where in your life you want God's power—you *need* God's power—but you're not experiencing God's power. Perhaps you are facing some kind of pressure, obstacle, temptation, opportunity, or challenge, and you have been praying and are wondering, *Why isn't God coming through for me?*

Could it be that you know the direction you need to be walking but you're sitting around waiting for God's power before you take the first step? Perhaps God is saying, *No. Show some faith. Get moving, get your feet wet, and I will give you power along the way.*

Why don't you take that first step and see what happens?

PONDER

Where in your life do you really need God's power?

PRACTICE

If you already had God's power in that area of your life, what would you do? Do it, in faith, expecting God to show up for you as you trust in him.

PRAY

God, I'm so impressed with your great power and I so need your great power. Please help me to act in faith, believing that you will give me the power I need as I trust in you.

CHAPTER 37

The Greatest Thing You'll Ever Do

No, in all these things we are more than conquerors through him who loved us. For I am convinced that neither death nor life, neither angels nor demons, neither the present nor the future, nor any powers, neither height nor depth, nor anything else in all creation, will be able to separate us from the love of God that is in Christ Jesus our Lord.
–Romans 8:37–39

As we enter into adulting, we wrestle with figuring out our unique path, how we'll contribute to the world, and what is the greatest thing we can do with our lives. Perhaps, like Anthony Victor of India, a retired headmaster known by his pupils as the "ear-haired teacher," you can enter the *Guinness Book of World Records*. Anthony has hair sprouting from his ears that measures 18.1 cm (7.12 inches) at its longest point.[1]

Excuses

I don't know what you want to accomplish with your life. (I hope it's not to have long ear hair. Gross!) Here's what I do know: so many people believe they *can't* do what they want to do. It's easy to make excuses. "I don't have what it takes." "My upbringing was too dysfunctional." "I don't know the right people." "I'm getting too late of a start on my dream." "My school loans are too much of a burden."

If you feel that way, I have good news. It's *really* good news. In fact, I'd encourage you to memorize what I'm about to tell you. It's just one sentence, but it's a good one, straight from the Bible, and it can literally change your perspective and your life. Here it is:

> No, in all these things we are more than conquerors through him who loved us. (Rom. 8:37)

No matter what you're facing, no matter the obstacles, not only can you overcome but you are *more* than a conqueror through him who loves you.

Get Up

In John 5, we see Jesus enter Jerusalem. Jerusalem was the holy city, the location of lots of holy places where many holy people hung out. Yet Jesus ignored all the "holiness" and headed straight for the pool of Bethesda. This pool was where all the not-so-holy people hung out. Hurting people gathered there, people who had lost hope and felt like they couldn't do what they wanted to do.

At the pool, Jesus met a man who had been paralyzed for thirty-eight years. Jesus asked him, "Do you want to get well?" (John 5:6). It's a simple question. A yes or no question. The man basically tells Jesus, "I can't, sir" and then gives some reasons why he's unable (see v. 7). *Not* what Jesus asked.

Jesus, ever gracious, ignores the man's victim mentality and tells him, "Get up! Pick up your mat and walk" (v. 8). From the man's perspective, standing up, picking up his mat, and walking were the three things he was unable to do.

The question then becomes, Will this man have the faith that through Jesus, he can overcome? Will he have the faith to try to do what Jesus was telling him to do?

The answer was yes. He stood up. He picked up his mat. He walked.

He discovered that "in all these things we are more than conquerors through him who loved us" (Rom. 8:37).

Whatever it is you feel Jesus is calling you to do, get up and do it. You can, because he loves you, and that means you're more than a conqueror.

No Excuses

I recently learned about a man named Erik Weihenmayer. At the age of fourteen he went blind. Can you imagine? Talk about having an excuse for feeling like you can't accomplish what you want to with your life! That's a good one.

Except Erik didn't use it as an excuse.

He wanted to wrestle, and he became a champion wrestler in high school.

He wanted to climb Mt. Everest, the highest mountain in the world, and he did that too. In fact, *Time* magazine did a cover story on his accomplishment. After he climbed Mt. Everest, someone told him, "Erik, don't let Everest be the greatest thing you ever do."[2]

He didn't. Erik went on to climb seven summits—the highest points on every continent. He's one of only 150 people to have ever done that, and he did it *blind*.

Today he speaks to and inspires large crowds around the world.

I don't know what you want to accomplish with your life. I don't know the greatest thing you could do. I *do* know that, no matter how you feel, there is no excuse holding you back. And if you feel like there is, I also know some really good news: in that very thing, you are more than a conqueror through him who loves you.

PONDER

Nothing can separate you from the love of God, and that love should compel you (see 2 Cor. 5:14). How can God's love give you permission and motivate you to go for it?

PRACTICE

God tells us to "write the vision" (Hab. 2:2 NKJV), and all kinds of modern research tells us that people who write down their goals are much more likely to accomplish them. Maybe it's time to write down what you want to accomplish with your life, believing that if it's God's will, through him you are more than able to do it.

PRAY

God, I am more than a conqueror because of you and your love. Please help me to believe that, don't let me forget it, and show me what it means to live my life according to that truth.

CHAPTER 38

The Power of Being Faithful

Therefore, my dear brothers and sisters, stand firm. Let nothing move you. Always give yourselves fully to the work of the Lord, because you know that your labor in the Lord is not in vain. –1 Corinthians 15:58

At The Porch, the young adult ministry I led for over a decade, we had hundreds of volunteers, but it was hard not to notice Kevin. He was the first to show up every week. He was the last to leave. He wasn't there to hang out and talk; he showed up to work. He wasn't trying to impress anyone, but he did. I started asking who he was. Soon, I was asking Kevin about himself. Eventually I discovered he was a talented writer. It all led to him getting a job as a copywriter at an advertising agency and to me hiring Kevin to help me with my writing projects (including coauthoring my first book, *Welcome to Adulting*).

When I think of Kevin, I think of the parable of the talents, which Jesus told, about three people who were trusted to steward some money. The two who proved faithful were then trusted with more.

The person who was not faithful was called "wicked" and lost all responsibility. It's like Jesus said in Luke 16:10, "Whoever can be trusted with very little can also be trusted with much, and whoever is dishonest with very little will also be dishonest with much." Kevin was faithful with a little, and now he's being trusted with much.

Insta-Life

The problem, I think, is that people today, especially young adults, value the instant: instant gratification, instant fame, and instant success. If you are not an internet billionaire by the time you are thirty, what have you been doing with your life?

In reality, though, it almost never works that way.

True gratification, true success, and true impact take time. But we are impatient and lose interest if we do not see instant results. We quit and move on to the next thing.

I think this highlights both the best and worst qualities of our generation. We think we can change the world, but we lack the long-term commitment to actually do so.

We overestimate what we can accomplish in a short period of time, which causes us to try but also to quit when it doesn't happen overnight. And we underestimate what we could get done if we faithfully pursued something for a long period of time.

One time at The Porch we talked about human trafficking, how slavery is still a rampant problem in our world. It was so exciting to see how people responded. They were ready to do something to be a solution to the problem. My fear was, Would they *stay* committed to being part of the solution?

Wilberforce

William Wilberforce lived in London two hundred years ago, when slavery was still legal. Though religious as a kid, by college he was known as a party animal who cared little for studying. (Sound familiar?) But a few years after college he returned to his faith. He truly committed to following Jesus wholeheartedly, even though at the time being an outspoken Christian was frowned upon in popular society. (Sound familiar?) Then he became aware of the huge problem of slavery and human trafficking and felt convicted that he had to do something about it. (Sound familiar?)

At the age of twenty-eight, he started a campaign against the slave trade. Slavery was legal and a big business. In fact, it was worth 80 percent of the country's foreign income.

Wilberforce gathered evidence and allies. He gave impassioned four-hour speeches. (He was a man after my own heart.) Finally, he presented a bill to Parliament. It failed. Big time. It was voted down by a 2–1 margin.

I think at that point most of us would have quit. "I tried but it didn't work." Nothing more would have come of it.

Not Wilberforce. He tried again the next year. He failed again. He tried again the next year. He failed again. He tried again the next year. He failed again. So he tried again . . . well, you get the picture.

After *twenty years* of faithful effort, he tried yet again . . . and succeeded. The slave trade was abolished.

Next he turned to the practice of slavery itself, and, after twenty-six more years it was abolished throughout the British Empire. This was in 1833, three decades before it was outlawed in the United

States. In fact, Abraham Lincoln gave credit to Wilberforce for moving the cause of abolition forward.

Only Forty-Six Years

It took Wilberforce only forty-six years to accomplish his goal.

My guess is you just read that last sentence and had a mini-stroke. "*Only* forty-six years? Forty-six *years*! Ain't nobody got time for that!"

If that was your reaction, you are missing the point. This guy took on big business, the status quo, the law, and the government—and he won. His actions resulted in eight hundred thousand people being freed from a lifetime of slavery. He changed his country, and the world, and it *only* took him forty-six years.

Whatever you want to accomplish with your life, the power to do it comes not in making a big splash or getting noticed but in faithfulness in the small things over the long haul.

If you are faithful, not because you want to be noticed but just because you want to be faithful, you will be noticed.

If you are faithful, not for a day because of a moment of inspiration but for years even if the result you want isn't happening, you will accomplish your goal.

Start now. Many people wait too long and then don't have forty-six years left to spend. The power of being a young adult is that you have time. Focus on what is truly important to you and be faithful.

People who try one thing after another, quitting each at the first failure—we don't talk about them two hundred years later. And the ones who spent forty-six solid years pursuing wealth, power, and fame? We don't talk about them either. The key is to focus on what is truly important and to be faithful. If you do that, you will find you have a power you did not realize you had.

PONDER

What do you want to accomplish with your life?

PRACTICE

What would it look like for you to be faithful in small things *today*? What is one perhaps small but faithful step you can take? Do it.

PRAY

God, I know you are always faithful to me, and I want to always be faithful to you. I want to do the right thing, even if it isn't currently producing the right result. Please help me to prove myself trustworthy, so you can trust me with more responsibility.

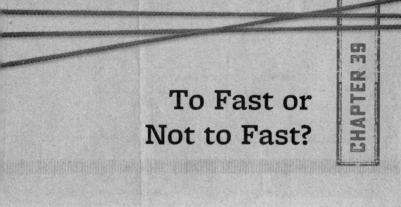

CHAPTER 39

To Fast or Not to Fast?

When you fast, do not look somber as the hypocrites do, for they disfigure their faces to show others they are fasting. Truly I tell you, they have received their reward in full. But when you fast, put oil on your head and wash your face, so that it will not be obvious to others that you are fasting, but only to your Father, who is unseen; and your Father, who sees what is done in secret, will reward you. –Matthew 6:16–18

I f we're talking about getting access to God's power, we have to talk about fasting. But fasting is not something we discuss much. If it's mentioned, I find people have lots of questions. "What is fasting? How do you fast? Why? Do I have to? Should I?"

What Is Fasting?

Biblical fasting is the act of giving up something—typically food—for a set period of time in order to draw closer to God.

Can You Fast from Just Certain Foods?

Though a typical fast means giving up all food, we see other variations in Scripture. Some fasts (see Esther 4:16 and Acts 9:9) involve abstaining from food and water. In those cases, the fast was limited to three days.

You can fast from food but still drink water. In Matthew 4, Jesus fasted for forty days. We're then told he was hungry, but not that he was thirsty. You can also fast from certain types of food. In Daniel 10:3, Daniel fasted from "choice food" for three weeks. It seems he did not have meat or wine but did have vegetables and water.

You can even fast from activities. First Corinthians 7:2–5 indicates that married couples may choose together to abstain from sex, "for a time, so that you may devote yourselves to prayer" (v. 5).

Some people choose to give up desserts, or television, or social media for a set amount of time. If the purpose is to focus more on God, this could also be considered a type of fast. But generally when people talk about fasting, they mean to give up all food for a specified amount of time.

Are Christians Required to Fast?

Fasting is not a requirement for salvation. It will not help you get into heaven.

In fact, nowhere in the Bible are Christians commanded to fast, but there is an expectation that we will. In Matthew 6:16–18, twice Jesus said, "when you fast." He assumes that we will fast.

In Matthew 9:14–15, Jesus explained that although his disciples weren't fasting while he was with them, soon he would be gone and "then they will fast." Again, Jesus endorsed fasting and seems to expect that his followers will fast.

Jesus doesn't command us to fast, but he endorses it and seems to expect it (and practiced it himself). It is an act of obedience and faithfulness, just like prayer or reading our Bible.

When Should You Fast?

There are works-based religions that require fasts at certain times of the year. Grace-based Christianity does not require such fasts. You have the freedom to fast or not fast whenever you want.

In the Bible, it was common for people to fast when seeking God's guidance on big decisions or before starting a new ministry (see Acts 13:2–3). David fasted as he prayed for his son to recover from an illness (see 2 Sam. 12:16) and to humble himself before the Lord (see Ps. 35:13). Ezra and Nehemiah fasted to confess and mourn sin (see Ezra 10:6 and Neh. 1:4–6). Jesus fasted while facing his temptation by Satan (see Matt. 4:1–4).

When should you fast? These examples would suggest doing so when you really need to seek God and access his wisdom and power.

How Long Should You Fast?

How long you fast is up to you. You can just skip a meal, or you can choose to not eat for days. Jesus fasted for forty days, and people today will sometimes fast that long. Bill Bright, the founder of Cru, fasted for forty days and has a guide to fasting you can find online.

Why Should You Fast?

What's the point of fasting? Again, God is the point. The purpose is to help you focus on God.

Choosing to give up food also proves, to yourself, how serious you are about talking to and listening for God.

The hunger pains you feel can serve as a recurring reminder that you have committed yourself to seeking God.

You will also have more time to pray, since you won't be eating and probably won't be cooking or doing dishes either.

Fasting can also help you overcome the need to control and help you exercise your trust in God. You will likely feel nervous going into a fast for the first time, or entering into a longer fast, and that's a good thing. It will force you to put your faith in God.

You will also find that fasting strengthens your resolve to overcome sin. When you are fasting, you are choosing to not follow your natural urges. You'll prove to yourself that, with God's help, you are capable of saying no even when you want to say yes.

PONDER

What excites you about fasting? What scares you about fasting?

PRACTICE

Pick a date, right now, to do (or start) some kind of fast that will help you focus on God.

PRAY

God, I want to know you, grow closer to you, and have your power in my life. If fasting will help me, lead me to fast. Make clear to me when you want me to fast, from what, and for how long.

CHAPTER 40

Live for Eternity

The kingdom of heaven is like treasure hidden in a field. When a man found it, he hid it again, and then in his joy went and sold all he had and bought that field. Again, the kingdom of heaven is like a merchant looking for fine pearls. When he found one of great value, he went away and sold everything he had and bought it. –Matthew 13:44–46

Tell me about your great-great-grandfather.

What did your great-great-grandfather do for a job? Did he have a car? What was a favorite hobby? How did he die?

Answers? I bet you don't know.

I've asked that question from stages around the world to thousands of young adults. I've asked it in small groups and in one-on-one conversations. Almost *no one* can tell me any details. In fact, the vast majority don't even know their great-great-grandfather's first name.

Think about that. If you're a young adult, young enough to have a living grandparent, odds are your great-great-grandfather was still alive about fifty years ago. This is not ancient history; it's just one generation before you were born. And we are not talking about some random person from history; this is your family member. You are his direct descendant. You would not be alive if it wasn't for him. And you don't know anything about him.

So, how will *you* be remembered?

You won't.

Fifty years after you are gone, your own great-great-grandkids won't even know your name. You will live. You will die. Shortly after, you will be forgotten. We all want to make our mark on the world; I'm sorry, but you won't.

> Surely the fate of human beings is like that of the animals; the same fate awaits them both: As one dies, so dies the other. All have the same breath; humans have no advantage over animals. Everything is meaningless. All go to the same place; all come from dust, and to dust all return. (Eccles. 3:19–20)

Eternity

If you won't be remembered for this life, what should you do? Choose not to live for this life. Live for eternity.

Think about eternity for a second. (That's an ironic sentence!) Imagine walking on a long, sandy beach. You take your finger and poke it in the sand. You pull it out and several grains of sand stick to it. You carefully brush all but one off. That single grain of sand represents your life. The entire beach represents eternity.

The Bible tells us that "we were born only yesterday and know nothing, and our days on earth are but a shadow" (Job 8:9). Your life is compared to "a passing breeze" (Ps. 78:39) and "a mist that appears for a little while and then vanishes" (James 4:14).

How do we respond? We should pray, "Show me, LORD, my life's end and the number of my days; let me know how fleeting my life is" (Ps. 39:4).

We should choose not to live for this life but to live for eternity.

Jesus told the story of a man who spent his life searching for something of true value. One day he finds a treasure hidden in a field. He realizes this is what he has been searching for his entire life. Everything else pales in comparison. In fact, he decides to sell *everything* so he can have this hidden treasure.

Jesus said that hidden treasure is the "kingdom of heaven." When you understand that heaven lasts for eternity and this life is just a grain of sand, you decide the only worthwhile pursuit is that which will last forever. Earthly riches and earthly fame are fleeting. You can fill your bank account with dollars or your Instagram account with followers, but it will all eventually turn to dust. But if you use your money to "store up for yourself treasures in heaven" (Matt. 6:20) and try to help other people become followers of Jesus, your impact will be eternal, and you will be rewarded forever.

PONDER

We are told, in Colossians 3:1–2, "Since, then, you have been raised with Christ, set your hearts on things above, where Christ is, seated at the right hand of God. Set your minds on things above, not on earthly things." How much of your time is spent thinking about "things above" (eternity, heaven) and how much is spent thinking about "earthly things" (popularity, success, vacations, getting more stuff)?

PRACTICE

Take a few minutes to prayerfully "audit" your life. Imagine a piece of paper divided into two sections: "earthly" and "eternity." You have to put everything in your life—your thoughts, desires, time spent, money spent, conversations, and so on—on one side or the other. Was it for/about life on earth or eternal life in heaven?

What does this audit say about what you are truly living for?

PRAY

God, help me to set my mind on things above. I want to think about and live for eternity. Help me to invest my time, talent, and treasure in the kingdom of heaven.

CHAPTER 41

Get in the Wheelbarrow

Trust in the LORD with all your heart and lean not on your own understanding; in all your ways submit to him, and he will make your paths straight. –Proverbs 3:5–6

My wife and kids and I go to a family camp every summer. This camp has a lake. Towering over the shore of the lake is the Screamer. You know the ginormous swing ride at the amusement park that takes you and swings you through the sky at incredible, heart palpitation–inducing rates of speed? The Screamer is nothing like that. Well, it does basically the same thing, but the Screamer looks like it was put together by a bunch of drunk rednecks as a torture device to scare their disobedient children into submission. It seems to be constructed from old PVC pipes and the remains of demolition cars and a burnt-down barn.

Every summer teenagers brag that they will go on the Screamer. Some chicken out, and others nearly lose their lunches being swung through the air and into the lake by the Screamer.

One summer my three-year-old announced she wanted to do it. I was told she would be the youngest rider ever. I was a proud dad.

The day came and she courageously walked up the six flights of stairs to get on the beast. At the top, she . . . freaked out. "Daddy, I can't do it. I can't do it. I can't do it." We proceeded to do the walk of shame *down* the six flights of stairs back to ground level.

The rest of the day everyone asked me, "Did she do it?" "No," I had to admit. "She got scared."

Ever feel that way?

The Phone Call

When I wrote my previous book, *Welcome to Adulting*, I was leading a young adult ministry that was growing exponentially. In fact, in addition to over four thousand people showing up every Tuesday night in person, we also had ten campuses around the world. Over fifty thousand people watched our services every week.

I also began to get more and more invitations. I was interviewed on *FOX News*. I was speaking at conferences and influential churches. I was given opportunities to speak in front of as many as four million people.

I noticed doors started opening. My meals were getting paid for. Honorariums for speaking went way up. I felt like I was handling it pretty well, but I knew the danger of what this could do to my heart. It was tempting to stop saying, "Look at Jesus," and start thinking, *Look at me.*

Right about that time I read a book called *Embracing Obscurity*. The (anonymous) author challenged readers to embrace obscurity for Jesus, to stop making much of ourselves so we can make much of him, to live for his glory and not our own.

Then I received a phone call. It was from the executive pastor of a church much smaller than the one I worked at. He told me they needed a new lead pastor and asked, "Do you know anyone good for this role?" I told him I would try to come up with some names for him. Then, in my quiet time with the Lord, I started to get a sense that it was me. I was confused.

I asked, "Really, God? Don't you want me to be as influential as I can be?"

I felt like God was telling me, *I don't need your platform, I need your faithfulness.*

It sounded crazy. I would have to take my kids out of school, sell our house, and move my family. Why? To go to a small town to become the pastor of a relatively small Baptist church in the middle of a field. I would be stepping out of the spotlight into obscurity. Honestly, it felt like career suicide. I was scared.

Ever felt that way?

You had a leading from God and sensed what he wanted you to do, but it felt like too much. It felt like more than you could handle. You wanted to, but . . . you were scared.

The Hall of Fame

Hebrews 11 is God's "Hall of Fame." It briefly tells the stories of the heroes of faith from the Old Testament of the Bible. Each hero's story begins with the words, "By faith." Each of their stories is filled with danger and risk. They were "living by faith" (Heb. 11:13). They believed in God enough to do what God was calling them to do. We're told in verse 6, "And without faith it is impossible to please God."

Faith is not just believing in God. Faith is trusting in God; trusting him enough to put your life in his hands.

The Wheelbarrow

You may have heard the oft-told story of "The Great Blondin." Charles Blondin was a famous French tightrope walker. On September 14, 1860, he became the first person to walk on a tightrope across Niagara Falls.

It's said that he walked across the falls, then crossed again on a bicycle, and then pushed across a wheelbarrow filled with potatoes. The crowd gathered to watch was amazed and shouted their approval. When Blondin reached the side of the river again, everyone cheered. He asked, "Do you believe I can carry a person across in this wheelbarrow?" The crowd roared, "Yes! We believe!" Blondin smiled, looked at a potential volunteer, and said, "Get in."

The person refused. *Everyone* refused. It is one thing to believe and another to trust enough to put your life in his hands.

The Decision

Remember how my daughter was too scared to ride the Screamer? In the days that followed, I talked to her about moving forward in the face of fear. I asked her, "Do you trust your daddy? Because I'm telling you, it is safe. I've got you. You can do this."

On the last day of camp, she said, "I trust you, Daddy. I want to do it." And she did. At three years old she rode the Screamer. And she *loved* it. For weeks, it was all she could talk about.

Remember how I was too scared to take the job at the smaller church in the middle of a field? In the days that followed I talked to God about moving forward in the face of fear. It's like I could hear him asking me, *Do you trust your daddy? Because I'm telling you, it is safe. I've got you. You can do this.*

As I wrote this book, I called that executive pastor back and told him I would take the job. We announced to my church that I was moving. Our house has gone up for sale.

I'm getting in the wheelbarrow. Will you?

Whatever it is you feel called to do, you can trust your heavenly Daddy.

PONDER

What do you feel God calling you to do but so far have been too scared to say yes to?

PRACTICE

Will you get in the wheelbarrow? What will that look like? Who should you tell?

PRAY

God, I want to walk by faith, not by sight. I know I cannot please you without faith. Help me to trust in you and not in my own understanding. Help me to do what you are calling me to do. I know you will make my paths straight. Thank you for loving me so much and for wanting to lead me into a bigger, better life. I pray in Jesus's name. Amen.

CHAPTER 42

A Day of Rest

> Therefore, since we are surrounded by such a great cloud of witnesses, let us throw off everything that hinders and the sin that so easily entangles. And let us run with perseverance the race marked out for us, fixing our eyes on Jesus, the pioneer and perfecter of faith. –Hebrews 12:1–2

This is the last day of our journey together, and your last day of rest. There's no reading, but I want to ask you to visualize something.

In Hebrews 11 we read about God's "Hall of Fame"—heroes of the faith. We are then told in the first verse of Hebrews 12 that they form a great cloud of witnesses who are rooting for us. They are watching.

We are then instructed to fix our eyes on Jesus. His example should inspire us.

As you continue to run the race marked out for you, visualize the crowd you have cheering you on, and Jesus who went before you, and be encouraged. God has a great plan for you, and you are not alone.

⭐ ACKNOWLEDGMENTS

There are so many people behind the work I do. God's incredible grace is often exemplified to me through the amazing people he allows me to partner with. First on the list is my beautiful wife, Monica. You are the kindest person I've ever met. You love as well as anyone I know. You disciple our kids, care for me, and are a friend to so many. I'll always love you, and I am more grateful than words can say that you choose to love me.

The kids we disciple, Presley, Finley, and Weston, keep us laughing and looking forward to the next adventure. Thank you for always letting me tell your stories. I know people think they know you, but your mamma and I know how truly wonderful you are. I pray for you daily that you would know the King, your Father in heaven.

My parents, Johnny and Laurie, taught me right from wrong. You taught me to prioritize the things of God. Mom, you were in the Word every morning, and Dad, you were on your knees beside your bed every night. This had a profound impact on my life. I am forever grateful for the ways you protected, guided, and provided for me, Amy, Scott, and Lisa.

My wife's parents, Jabo and Caroline, are the best in-laws anyone could ask for. You gave me the amazing partner in ministry that I have in my bride. You also gave me a real friend in your son, Matt. We are "ride or die" brothers. Thank you for the ways you invest in our family and care so well for me!

Todd Wagner and the elders of Watermark sent me through a twelve-year "university" on leadership. You guys have prepared me so well for the future, and you were always ready and willing to invest in the next generation. You guys get it. Thank you, Todd, for how much you have given me over the years. Thank you also for believing in me when you shouldn't have. I pray that you continue to see a kingdom return on your investment in me.

Our new Harris Creek family has been so welcoming. Your kindness toward our family will never be forgotten. I am so excited to fight evil, exalt Jesus, experience community, and seek the welfare of our city with you! I am thankful for our elders and staff for carrying this church forward. As you love the Lord with all your heart, there is no limit to how he will use us to help everyone follow Jesus.

Young adults are the future of the church. Whether you call yourself Gen Y, Gen Z, Millennials, or anything else, you are the future. As you seek God you will find him. He is real. He loves you. He desires to use you in ways you can't even imagine. Prioritize getting to know him. Do more of what makes you love him. Stop doing things that distract you from him. You are the future, and as you do these things, the future is *bright*!

 **NOTES**

Chapter 4 Questions to Ask When Navigating a Gray Area

1. I was given these questions years ago but don't know their original source. They may have been originally put together by John MacArthur. See John MacArthur, "What to Do in the Gray Areas," *Grace to You*, July 4, 2009, https://www.gty.org/library/articles/A332/what-to-do-in-the-gray-areas.

Chapter 5 Undulation

1. C. S. Lewis, *The Screwtape Letters* (San Francisco: HarperSanFrancisco, 2001), 37–38.

Chapter 9 Compounding Interest

1. C. S. Lewis, *Mere Christianity* (New York: Macmillan, 1943), 117.

Chapter 11 Here's a Tip

1. E. W. Dunn et al., "Spending Money on Others Promotes Happiness," *Science*, May 29, 2009, https://www.ncbi.nlm.nih.gov/pubmed/18356530.

Chapter 13 The Power of Habits

1. Charles Duhigg, *The Power of Habit: Why We Do What We Do in Life and Business* (New York: Random House, 2012).

2. James Clear, *Atomic Habits* (New York: Avery, 2018).

3. Oswald Chambers, "Get Moving: June 15," *My Utmost for His Highest* (Grand Rapids: Discovery House, 1992).

Chapter 15 The Lonely Generation

1. Aaron Smith, "6 New Facts about Facebook," Pew Research Center, February 3, 2014, http://www.pewresearch.org/fact-tank/2014/02/03/6-new-facts -about-facebook/.

2. Miller McPherson et al., "Social Isolation in America: Changes in Core Discussion Networks over Two Decades," *American Sociological Review*, June 2006, http://journals.sagepub.com/doi/abs/10.1177/000312240607100301.

3. Jo Griffin, "The Lonely Society," *The Mental Health Foundation*, 2010, https:// www.mentalhealth.org.uk/sites/default/files/the_lonely_society_report.pdf; M. Luhmann and L. C. Hawkley, "Age Differences in Loneliness from Late Adolescence to Oldest Old Age," *Developmental Psychology*, June 2016, https://www .ncbi.nlm.nih.gov/pubmed/27148782.

4. "2011 Relationships Indicators Survey," *Relationships Australia*, 2011, http://www.rasa.org.au/media-centre/relationships-indicator-survey-2011/#.

5. Liz Mineo, "Good Genes Are Nice, but Joy Is Better," *Harvard Gazette*, April 11, 2017, https://news.harvard.edu/gazette/story/2017/04/over-nearly-80 -years-harvard-study-has-been-showing-how-to-live-a-healthy-and-happy-life/.

6. Elizabeth Bernstein, "Why Our Mental Health Takes a Village," *Wall Street Journal*, January 22, 2018, https://www.wsj.com/articles/why-our-mental-health -takes-a-village-1516640136.

Chapter 20 Time to Commit

1. Grace Murano, "World's Longest," *Oddee*, October 5, 2009, https://www .oddee.com/item_96837.aspx.

Chapter 22 Clearness Committee

1. Bronnie Ware, *The Top Five Regrets of the Dying: A Life Transformed by the Dearly Departing* (Carlsbad, CA: Hay House, 2012).

2. Sara Burrows, "85% of People Hate Their Jobs, Gallup Poll Says," *Return to Now*, September 22, 2017, https://returntonow.net/2017/09/22/85-people-hate -jobs-gallup-poll-says/.

3. Parker Palmer, *Let Your Life Speak* (San Francisco: Jossey-Bass, 2000), 16.

4. Palmer, *Let Your Life Speak*, 16.

Chapter 23 Growing Young

1. As quoted in Ravi Zacharias, *Can Man Live without God?* (Nashville: Thomas Nelson, 2004), 88.

Chapter 24 I Choose Contentment

1. "Ted Turner," InvesterarCitat.se, accessed March 26, 2019, http://www .investerarcitat.se/popularast-just-nu/ted-turner/.

2. Patrick Morley, *A Man's Guide to Work: 12 Ways to Honor God on the Job* (Chicago: Moody, 2010), 95.

Chapter 25 Before You Face Your Giant

1. As quoted in Bryan M. Chavis, *Buy It, Rent It, Profit!: Make Money as a Landlord in ANY Real Estate Market* (New York: Simon & Schuster, 2009), 56.

Chapter 29 Worried for No Reason

1. Ronald C. Kessler et al., "The Global Burden of Mental Disorders: An Update from the WHO World Mental Health (WMH) Surveys," *Epidemiologia e Psichiatria Sociale* 18, no. 1 (Jan–Mar 2009): 23–33, https://www.ncbi.nlm.nih .gov/pubmed/19378696.

2. Norman B. Anderson et al., "Stress in America: Paying with Our Health," *American Psychological Association*, February 4, 2015, https://www.apa.org/news /press/releases/stress/2014/stress-report.pdf.

3. T. M. Luhrmann, "The Anxious Americans," *New York Times*, July 18, 2015, https://www.nytimes.com/2015/07/19/opinion/sunday/the-anxious-americans .html.

4. Tom C. Russ et al., "Association between Psychological Distress and Mortality: Individual Participant Pooled Analysis of 10 Prospective Cohort Studies," *BMJ*, July 31, 2012, http://www.bmj.com/content/345/bmj.e4933.

Chapter 30 The Antidote for Anxiety

1. Tony Jones, *The Sacred Way* (El Cahon, CA: Youth Specialties, 2005), 79.

Chapter 37 The Greatest Thing You'll Ever Do

1. "Longest Ear Hair," *Guinness Book of World Records*, accessed April 16, 2019, http://www.guinnessworldrecords.com/world-records/longest-ear-hair.

2. Interview with Rae Williams, "No Barriers: Erik Weihenmayer," *Author Hour with Rae Williams*, September 21, 2017, https://www.authorhour.co/erik -weihenmayer-no-barriers/.

Jonathan "JP" Pokluda came to understand the grace of the gospel in his early twenties after being involved in different denominational churches his entire life. This ignited a desire in him to inspire young adults to radically follow Jesus Christ and unleash them to change the world. His first book, *Welcome to Adulting*, offers Millennials a roadmap to navigating faith, finding a spouse, friendships, finances, and the future.

JP led The Porch for over a decade. Under his leadership, God grew The Porch to be the largest ministry to young adults of its kind, with tens of thousands listening weekly around the world. Recently JP and his family moved to Waco, Texas, to pastor a group of believers called Harris Creek. He still ministers to young adults through speaking, writing, and his weekly podcast, *Becoming Something*. JP's partner in ministry is his wife of fourteen years, Monica, and together they disciple their children, Presley, Finley, and Weston.

JONATHAN POKLUDA

CONNECT WITH JP

Jonathan Pokluda | @JPokluda | JPokluda
HarrisCreek | @HarrisCreek | Harris_Creek

Dear world-changer,

First, I want to sincerely thank you for investing in this book. While there are many trials today, when I think about the future of the church I am very hopeful. I believe that God is preparing you for such a time as this. One of the concerns that I have for the church is our worship of people and "celebrity pastors." I want you to know that I would much rather you follow Jesus than me. With that said, I still love to connect with other Jesus followers, and I am always encouraged by hearing about what God is doing through young adults around the world. If you'd like to connect, there are some tools above that can help! I am praying for you as I write this, that you are connected to a local Bible-teaching church, and if you are ever in Waco, please come and say "hi" at Harris Creek Baptist Church.

Adulting with you,

Jonathan Pokluda

Want the book that SPARKED this survival guide?

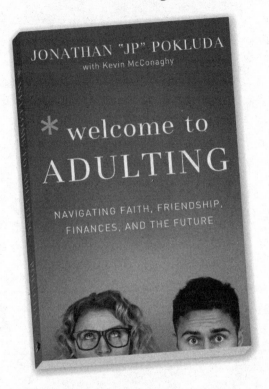

Combining entertaining stories from his own experience, insights from the Bible, and compelling evidence from research, Jonathan "JP" Pokluda lays out a roadmap in *Welcome to Adulting* for how to navigate your life as an adult.

LIKE THIS
BOOK?

Consider sharing
it with others!

- Share or mention the book on your social media platforms.
  Use the hashtag **#WelcometoAdultingSurvivalGuide**

- Write a book review on your blog or on a retailer site.

- Pick up a copy for friends, family, or anyone who you think
  would enjoy and be challenged by its message!

- Share this message on Twitter, Facebook, or Instagram:
  **I loved #WelcometoAdultingSurvivalGuide by
  @JPokluda // @ReadBakerBooks**

- Recommend this book for your church, workplace,
  book club, or class.

- Follow Baker Books on social media and tell us what you like.

 **ReadBakerBooks**

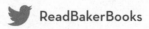 **ReadBakerBooks**

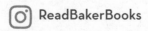 **ReadBakerBooks**